Discovering Banff
Moray & Nairn

GW00600590

Discovering
Banff
Moray & Nairn

ERIC SIMPSON

JOHN DONALD PUBLISHERS LTD
EDINBURGH

To my daughter Rhona
and sons Fraser and Moray.

ISBN 0 85976 329 3

British Library Cataloguing in Publication Data
A catalogue record for this book
is available from the British Library.

Phototypeset by The Midlands Book Typesetting Company,
Loughborough.
Printed & bound in Great Britain by Bath Press, Bath.

Contents

Acknowledgements

I am indebted first and foremost to my wife Kathleen for reading the text and for her many helpful suggestions. My son, Fraser, is due my thanks for developing and printing my photographs. Many other people have helped in a variety of ways. They include Dorothy Kidd, Jean Mackenzie, Alan G. McQuaker, the Earl of Moray, Harold and Mary Reid, Veronica Gordon Smith and Sandy Walker. I am grateful too for the help provided by the staff of many different libraries, museums and archive repositories. Since I have consulted hundreds of books and articles, I am obviously indebted to the historians and other writers of the past and also to many contemporary researchers. Articles and books written by Mr G. A. Dixon and Mr M. Seton (of Moray District Libraries) have been of particular value. I have profited too from the many publications of the splendidly prolific Moray District Libraries and also from the standard histories such as the Edinburgh History of Scotland and the New History of Scotland. A few of the works I have consulted are mentioned in the text and a selection of the others is listed below in the Further Reading section. Lastly, let me express my gratitude to the adult students who attended my Edinburgh University Extra-mural classes on the history of the north-east and who thereby helped me to maintain my enthusiasm for this project.

Introduction

Scotland in miniature! This is in many ways a not inapt description of the three historic counties of Banff, Moray and Nairn, except, of course, that they lack big towns and industrial cities. But, like Scotland as a whole, the three north-east counties incorporate both a considerable mountainous area and an extensive, richer lowland zone. This Scotland in microcosm is certainly a land of contrasts, extending from the Moray Firth coastal plain in the north to the snow-capped Cairngorms in the south. The upland zone is truly Highland — 'land of the mountain and the flood' — embracing some of the highest peaks in Scotland. Lonely Loch Avon (pronounced A'an) and the Shelter Stone, that erstwhile reivers' den, lie within the bounds of the old county of Banff. At its southern extremity, the auld county boundaries reach to the summits of Cairngorm and of mighty Ben Macdhui; they touch too the North Top of Beinn A'Bhuird and the summit tor of many-topped Ben Avon.

In the upland fastnesses of the three counties the old-time smugglers made the 'real Glenlivet' and other home-distilled whiskies. Now, while walkers and pony-trekkers follow the smugglers' tracks of yesteryear, car and bus-borne tourists take waymarked whisky trails which lead to far-famed Speyside malt whisky distilleries. The name whisky as well as much of the product is Highland, since it derives from uisge beatha, which is Gaelic for the water of life. The many Gaelic place-names that are still in use, albeit sometimes in altered form, also serve as a reminder that this form of Celtic speech was in its time the tongue of the dominant elite and was, until the 19th century, still fairly widely spoken in the upland parishes of Banff, Moray and Nairn. From these uplands flow, in a south-westerly direction, the principal rivers — the Nairn, the Findhorn, the Spey and the Deveron, which, at their best, are fine rivers to fish, giving the kind of sport which has helped to turn the whole area into a sportman's paradise.

In the Laich o Moray and elsewhere in the lowland plain —

a landscape with its own quiet appeal — there is fertile soil and, accordingly, there are many good farms. There are, in lowlands and highlands alike, numerous defiantly-imposing castles and many other buildings of great historical and architectural interest — the most famous being Elgin Cathedral, the once glorious 'Lantern of the North'. The rich farmlands of the lowland zone helped to support royal burghs like Forres, Elgin and Banff, whose street patterns even today demonstrate their medieval origins. Over the centuries other towns and villages were built. Many of them date from the 18th and early 19th centuries, when numerous neat and regularly-laid-out planned villages were constructed. On the often spectacular Moray Firth coastline there is contrast, too, ranging from old-world, brightly-painted fishing touns to busy ports and douce, seaside resorts. These different places, in their individual ways, have appealed to discerning visitors from the 18th century to the present day.

Moray itself has a long history as an identifiable area. In the early Middle Ages the Mormaers (or overlords) of Moray ruled a mighty province which stretched from east of the Spey to the Sound of Sleat. Later the counties emerged. Beginning as medieval royal sheriffdoms they evolved, after a long period of time, into democratically elected organs of local government. They took their modern form with elected councils as late as 1890. In 1975 however, following local government reorganisation, the ancient counties were dismembered. Banffshire as such disappeared, the eastern part helping to form the newly-created District of Banff and Buchan. The western area went to Moray District which, with Banff and Buchan, formed part of the also newly-established Grampian Region. On the other hand, Grantown and a large chunk of south-west Morayshire were transferred to Badenoch and Strathspey in Highland Region. Since Grantown had been part of the Highland county of Inverness-shire until 1870, this was in a way an administrative reversal. Moray and Nairn, which had been put together — for some functions only — in 1930, were divorced in 1975, when Nairn District was constituted and also allocated to Highland Region. Nevertheless, the historic counties of Banff, Moray and Nairn had a long history as distinct administrative units and this simple fact cannot be expunged from the historical record. Whether the present local government system will last so long

Ben Avon — the 'magical' granite tor of Clach-na-Bhan (the women's stone — description on pages 16 and 17). (Photograph: Fraser Simpson)

is rather doubtful, the more especially since now, 17 years after the last reorganisation, further far-reaching changes are under active consideration.

In this short study, I have tried to survey the key events, issues and developments that, for better or worse, have shaped the history of the three counties. Over the centuries there have been wars and battles — some caused by foreign invaders, others the consequence of local feuds and rivalries. Not of course that the north-east, and Scotland in general, were different from other countries in these respects. Those who assert that the Scots have had a particularly bloody history have scant awareness of the divisions and troubles that have plagued other European countries. Like the free foresters described in chapter 11, I have done some poaching, inasmuch as I have, on occasion, strayed outwith the boundaries of the three counties for the sake of the storyline and also to present a more coherent picture. On the other hand, due to insufficient space and my own lack of expertise, I have, I confess, neglected some important facets of the local heritage — the counties' rich musical tradition for instance.

Information on these and other aspects of the area may be elicited from the various local libraries, museums and other visitor centres. The District Tourist Boards, for instance, provide a wealth of helpful information sheets and leaflet-guides, many of which are, contrary to the stereotype of the canny Scot, supplied free of charge.

The Old Counties

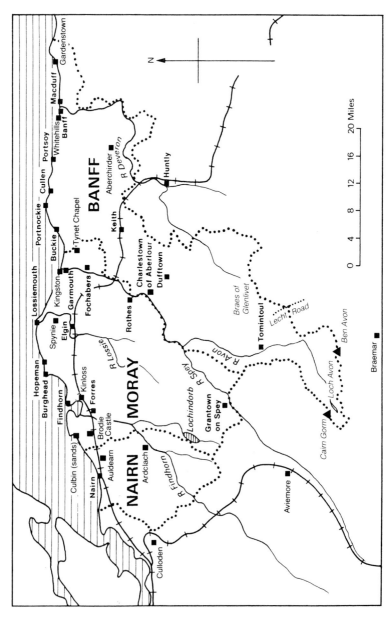

Location Map

CHAPTER 1

Ancient Peoples and Ancient Traditions

'The silent vanished races'

Every now and again ancient stone arrow-heads are turned up by the plough or the spade. In the not too distant past country-folk in the north-east, like indeed their counterparts elsewhere in Europe, called them elf-bolts or fairy-shots. This belief survived in Fordyce parish at least until the 1790s. Coming, as many people believed, from arrows shot by fairies, they were thereby thought to be imbued with magical properties and were sometimes worn as amulets — to provide protection against the fairies or other misfortunes and also to cure disease.

In reality the elf-bolts of popular superstition were the arrow-heads of stone-age hunters. The makers and users of such weapons were nomadic hunters and food-gatherers, who moved into the area some 9,000 thousand years ago. They are the earliest inhabitants for whom we have clear evidence. What had been inhospitable territory at the time of the last Ice Age became habitable as the climate improved. Tempted north by an abundance of game, these nomads probably followed migrating wild animals and were, therefore, constantly on the move. Traces of their camp-sites have been found at a number of locations, including the Culbin Sands near Findhorn. The early stone age hunters (or Mesolithic people in archaeologists' parlance) made tiny but sharp spear-points and arrow-heads from flint, chert or quartz. Being really minuscule, it is perhaps not surprising that the arrow-heads and other projectiles of this period were attributed to the fairies.

From around 4000 BC there is evidence that a new race had arrived. As the land was then densely wooded, it is likely that the neolithic (or New Stone Age) newcomers took the sea route north, sailing their dug-out canoes and skin-covered boats fairly close to the shore. While, like their precursors, the technologically more advanced newcomers fished and hunted

and gathered fruits and berries, they were first and foremost
farmers — herding animals and growing crops. Neolithic,
or new Stone Age, men dug for flint at a flint mine at
Boddam in Buchan for the scrapers, knives and other tools
that they required for themselves or for barter. As tillers of
the soil, they lived in settled communities, dwelling in huts
whose surface traces have long since vanished. Fortunately
some of their burial-vaults, erected for what presumably were
the leading families, have proved more durable. And, being
built as artificial mounds, they are certainly easier to find.
Archaeologists call them chambered tombs because the human
remains of many generations were placed in a stone-built inner
chamber which was covered by an earthen barrow or a cairn of
stones. Some of these monumental burial-places, like the aptly
named Longmanhill cairn (two miles south-east of Macduff),
were built on a prominent site. Like some castles and kirks
of more recent centuries, they were evidently raised on high
as potent symbols of the status and authority of the builders.
It is likely, too, that they served as ritualistic centres. As with
the so-called elf-arrows, these seemingly mysterious mounds
and barrows, which we now know to be neolithic, aroused the
curiosity of later generations. What Robert Louis Stevenson so
graphically depicted as 'the howes of the silent vanished races'
were explained away as fairy knowes or, equally erroneously,
as the graves of Danes or of kings and other warriors slain
in battle.

The north-east is noted for a distinctive type of chambered
cairn, called by archaeologists Clava cairns because the most
impressive examples are those at Clava in Inverness-shire.
Distinctive from having a circle of standing stones erected
round them, the Clava burial cairns, which lie between the
battlefield of Culloden and the River Nairn, fall into two
categories. Some are called ring cairns, because they have no
ground-level entrance. When human remains were inserted,
entry was made from above. Others, however, had an entrance
passage leading to a central burial area. Whereas, with other
types of passage cairn the entrance usually faces east or
south-east, the Clava cairn passages are oriented towards the
south-west. At Clava the passages point to the setting sun at
the time of the winter solstice.

In upper Speyside within Moray District there are three Clava cairns fairly close to each other near Bridge of Avon, Ballindalloch. Two are at Lagmore, the western one, which is on an elevated site, being the more impressive. Although comparatively little remains of the eastern cairn, it, with five surviving standing stones, lies close to the A95 (on the south side) and can be viewed from the road. Just over a mile away, if following the road to Aberlour, a track going left towards the Spey leads to a ring cairn. The circle and inner cairn here are in an enclosed wooded area. The highest of the five stones in this circle, which is 2.74 metres high, can be seen behind the dyke which forms the enclosure. Set into this dyke is one of the smaller stones — a neat example of adaptation. Built by people who must have treated their ancestors with great reverence, these post-3000 BC chambered tombs were used for funeral and other ritualistic ceremonies over a long period of time.

But there are other sacred or ritualistic centres which also belong to the neolithic period. Standing stones, for example, are to be found at a variety of locations — erected, it must be presumed, for ceremonial purposes and, as with the Clava cairns, probably also to provide astronomical sightlines. Many stone circles and other standing stones were, it seems, aligned with prominent features on the horizon at times of astronomic significance. The moment when the sun or moon or a very bright star set or rose on the predicted line of sight would have been the crucial time for the neolithic sky-watchers.

An interesting stone circle, or rather the remnants of one, can be seen in the eastern part of Moray District at Rothiemay. There are four conventional standing stones — one with intriguing pecked designs or cupmarks. In addition, however, there is also a massive stone slab, also cupmarked, which has been set on its side. Because of this latter feature, this type of monument, which is unique to the north-east, is known as a recumbent stone circle.

Stone circles were regarded with reverence or awe by later peoples — most certainly by the dominant groups in what for convenience may be called the Bronze Age. Countryfolk, too, in more recent centuries had their own theories and ways of explaining such relics of a far distant and mysterious past. 'St Marnan's Chair' is the traditional name for a monolith that can be viewed at the old Marnoch kirk, which is three miles south-west of Aberchirder and another three (as the crow flies) from Rothiemay. By Bankhead to the south of Portsoy a recumbent stone circle was known to the locals as 'St Brandan's Stanes'. While standing stones were often misleadingly called Druidical temples, in the case of a stone circle north of the Moray village of Urquhart, its name, 'The Deil's Stanes', suggests an origin of quite a different character. An alternative name for this circle 'The Nine Stanes' is unfortunately no longer valid as only five uprights remain. It is to be regretted that 'improving' lairds and farmers removed so many of these ancient relics. At least one standing stone which had been removed was subsequently restored. This is a lofty stone at Auchorachan in Glenlivet which was returned to its original position, after the farmer responsible for shifting it had become 'troubled'. Sadly, as recently as 1976, a long barrow at Bank of Roseisle in Moray was removed for agricultural improvements.

Stone circles and related monuments continued to serve some role or function in the age when metal came into use. On the other hand, burial practices changed with interments in small slab-built cists being a feature of what in traditional chronology is termed the Beaker Period or early Bronze Age. Within each cist a corpse was placed — laid on its side in a crouched, foetal-like position. Quite a few of these stone cists had been covered by a round mound, usually a cairn. Many also contained grave-goods including beakers and other distinctive forms of pottery. Since the skulls found in beaker graves are markedly different (being broader and shorter) than those from chambered cairns, it is likely that there was an influx of new immigrants at that time.

In the late Bronze Age (from circa 1600 BC) personal display must have counted for a great deal. This was true not only in life but also in death, as precious and other prestigious objects have been retrieved from the graves of high-caste members of that society. Valuable finds of this period include a number of jet necklaces and an unusual pair of gold ornaments. These, which some have considered to be earrings and others hair ornaments, were uncovered at Orbliston in 1863. Dug up by railway navvies, probably from a short cist, they passed

'St Marnan's Chair' — at Old Marnoch Church. This kirk, built in 1792, was the scene of the protests described in chapter 7. (Photograph: the author)

through several hands and just escaped being melted down. While one was subsequently lost, the other is now in the Royal Scottish Museum in Edinburgh. A replica can be seen at Elgin Museum, which, incidentally, has very well laid out displays of archaeological and historical artefacts. In the 18th and 19th centuries it was common practice for lairds with an antiquarian bent to dig into the often conspicuously sited Bronze Age mounds. Sometimes it was intellectual curiosity that motivated them, but more often perhaps it was in hope of finding buried treasure. Quite a number of cairns were needlessly destroyed. This was the fate of the Core Stanes in the parish of Rathven. When the laird of Letterfourie biggit a new hoose in 1773, he used the stones from this remarkable cairn for his Adam-designed mansion. In the second half of the 19th century some enthusiastic amateurs, drawn from the ranks of the business and professional classes, embarked on excavations. Some of these amateurs indeed proved to be very competent investigators. Although some of their finds passed into private collections and subsequently disappeared, many were donated to local museums and therefore can still be seen and studied. Of the Victorian antiquarians my favourite is an iconoclastic Buckie 'gentleman of character' who, in addition to various 'antediluvian' relics, claimed to have acquired 'a feather of the cock that crew at Peter.'

Excavations in caves have led to interesting finds, such as tools for leatherworking and valuable ornaments unearthed at the 'Sculptor's Cave' at Covesea on the shore east of Hopeman. With access limited by tides, this cave may have been utilised as a refuge in times of danger. This particular cave has a history of occupation and/or use over a very long time. Its name, the 'Sculptor's Cave', derives indeed from symbols incised on the walls by Pictish occupants in the Early Christian period.

Going back to the late Bronze Age, the fact that many weapons have been found indicate that this was a period of conflict and war. The likely cause for this state of affairs was climatic deterioration which led to the abandoning of previously cultivated upland areas. From around 1400 BC the peoples who lived on marginal hill-farms had to endure repeated crop failure. Apart from more emphasis on stock-raising, the major consequence was pressure on, and competition for, life-sustaining resources such as valuable livestock and the remaining cultivable land. With the main economic base for late Bronze Age and Iron Age societies being cattle and other livestock, the need to protect the human and animal population led to the building of fortifications. It was in the Iron Age (circa 600 BC to AD 100) that the first hill-top forts were erected as, for example, the Doune of Relugas (on the Forres to Grantown road) and Little Conval by Dufftown. But why the latter fort was left unfinished remains a puzzle. The Victorians' obsession with the Druids ensured that this defensive structure was considered to be their handiwork.

Sadly a fortification at Kinneddar, just south of Lossiemouth, which may well have dated back to this time was destroyed by an 18th-century agricultural improver. Likewise razed to the ground was the medieval castle which had been built within the ramparts of the older fort — a remarkable instance of continuity of function.

There were also coastal promontory forts at Burghead, Portnockie, and Cullykhan; and these too show continuity of use over a long period of time. The defensive value of the site at Castle Point at Cullykhan Bay (which is west of Pennan) was appreciated by the native peoples from the late Bronze Age to the 18th century. The defences of the early Iron Age period (circa 400 BC) on this sea-girt promontory comprised a wall of stone and timber with an elaborate gateway. A later defensive wall, which had been laced with timber, proved vulnerable and was destroyed by fire. As to when and by whom we can only conjecture. As happened at similar timber-laced forts, the great heat engendered, following the firing of the walls, fused or vitrified the stonework.

The warrior aristocracy of the Iron Age displayed their wealth and power in ostentatious ways wearing, for example, heavy bronze armlets. A snake armlet found at the Culbin Sands is a splendid example of what seems to have been a north-eastern speciality. The mouthpiece of a war trumpet is another relic of this age of tribal conflict. This mouthpiece, which is in the form of a boar's head, was found at Deskford in the last century and is now held by the Royal Scottish Museum in Edinburgh. The sound of war trumpets like this would have been heard when tribe fought tribe and perhaps, too, when a new and very formidable foe threatened the power of the Celtic warlords of northern Britain.

The new major enemy that made its presence felt were the Roman legions which under the command of Julius Agricola invaded Scotland. A confederacy of northern tribes resisted the invaders. This confederacy which the Romans identified as the Caledonians was defeated around 84 AD at the battle of Mons Graupius. A number of different sites have been proposed for the site of this battle including Bennachie in Aberdeenshire and the Pass of Grange near Keith in Banffshire. It is likely that Roman marching camps in both these areas relate to Agricola's campaign. Other camps may belong to the early third century when the Emperor Severus led a major expedition which reached far into Scotland. The process of discovery goes on, and some archaeologists regard two sites first revealed by aerial survey as probable Roman encampments. These are Easter Galcantray near Cawdor and Balnageith between Forres and the River Findhorn. If confirmed, the latter would be the most northerly Roman fortification. The absence of any permanent forts reminds us that, while they may have been defeated in the field by the disciplined and superbly trained and equipped Romans, the peoples of the north remained unconquered.

One legacy of the Roman incursions is that we can begin to give names to places and peoples. The 'silent peoples' of the distant past are silent no more. We can identify, albeit tentatively, place-names such as Loxa (River Lossie) and Tuensis (River Spey). Classical writers from the third century AD onward refer to the Picts as being the people who dominated Scotland north of the Forth. While there are enormous blanks in our knowledge about the Picts, there is little doubt that the dominant language in the north was a Celtic tongue akin to Welsh. Although the surviving written record is minimal, their artistic achievements, particularly their craftsmanship in stone, were of a very high order. In Banff, Moray and Nairn there are many examples of Pictish carved stones which bear symbols that have intrigued and puzzled scholars over a long period of time. Some of these stones will be referred to in other contexts.

For the Picts the afore-mentioned promontory forts at Cullykhan, Burghead and at Portnockie (Green Castle) were centres of power and authority. Burghead indeed may have been at least a regional capital. Although very much was destroyed when a new planned settlement was built in the early 19th century, 18th-century maps and records show that the promontory's defences included on the landward side a triple set of massive ramparts and ditches. Archaeological investigators have shown that there were two inner enclosures which were protected by a stone-faced wall. The core of the wall was laced with timber. This constructional technique was one that the Picts inherited from their Bronze and Iron Age ancestors and predecessors and one too that they long continued to employ, as for instance at Green Castle along the coast at Portnockie. This particular timber-laced promontory fort may well have been built to meet the threat from Viking invaders.

Within the inner wall of the Burghead fort there is an amazing well with worn stone steps leading down to a deep rock-cut inner chamber. While the Burghead well obviously had a very practical function, it is reasonable to assume that such an elaborately fashioned structure had some symbolic significance for the Picts and/or their precursors. One thing is certain. It is not, as was once asserted, a Roman well. Likewise symbolic — serving as a totem for a local tribal group or symbolising perhaps the power and authority of a Pictish warlord — are the stone bull carvings of Burghead. Incised on slabs and pieces of stones, the six surviving bull carvings (including two in the public library of Burghead and two in Elgin museum) date most likely from the 7th century. Two centuries or so later this Pictish stronghold was destroyed but why and by whom is another of the many tantalising puzzles of the so-called Dark Age period.

While from around 800 AD the Vikings posed a major threat to the Picts of the north-east lowlands, the absence of Scandinavian place-names, unlike, for example, Lewis and the Northern Isles, indicates that the Northmen were in the long term at least successfully repulsed. Around 844 AD the Picts indeed did have to submit to outside rule but their new overlord was not a Viking but Kenneth MacAlpin, King of Dal Riata. From then on Scots and Picts were united but the Scots of

Pitchroy on the Speyside Way near Ballindalloch. 'Pit' means a share of land; the second element is the Gaelic 'chruaidh' meaning hard. (Photograph: the author)

Dal Riata were supreme in the new Kingdom of Alba. The Picts of the north-east lost their independent identity, and the very great number of Gaelic place-names throughout the area reflect the political and linguistic dominance of the Gaelic-speaking Scots. Indeed even 'Pit' place-names, though clearly identified with areas that were part of the Pictish heartland, provide pointers to the eastward migration of Scots from Dal Riata. In place-names like Pitgaveny, Pitchroy, Pittyvaich and Pitglassie the second elements are Gaelic in origin. 'Pit' means a share of land, so Pitcraigie (at Rothes) describes a craggy or rocky piece of land. Scholarly opinion suggests that such place-names derive from settlements established in newly cleared forest by Scots who migrated to the east in the second half of the 9th century.

One common factor that may have promoted assimilation and eased the path to union was the common acceptance by Picts and Scots of the Christian faith. There is testimony in stone to the spread of Christianity inasmuch as, while the earliest Pictish carvings show only symbols whose purpose

Pictish symbols on Rodney's Stone in Brodie Castle grounds. This sculptured stone, which has a cross on the reverse side, was unearthed when foundations were being dug for Dyke Kirk. (Photograph: the author)

and meaning are obscure, the later ones show a very marked Christian influence.

It is noteworthy too that the early evangelists came to the north-east from the west, beginning with St Columba's missionary visit to King Brudei of the Picts around 565 AD. While Brudei, whose capital was at or near Inverness, was impressed by Columba's magical powers, the conversion of the northern Picts was a long-term process and owed more to the activities of later missionaries. Although not conclusive evidence, church dedications provide some pointers to the presence of Celtic holy men who, during the 7th and 8th centuries, followed in Columba's tracks and carried the Christian faith from Iona and other western monastic centres. While there are many dubious attributions, dedications to St Moluag of Lismore at Mortlach (modern Dufftown) and St Maelrubha at Keith and Rafford could well indicate the presence of early evangelists in the Columban tradition.

The crosses carved on some later Pictish stones bear silent testimony to the impact of Christianity. While there is debate about the origins and purpose of the symbols that adorn, for example, one side of Rodney's Stone (which can be seen at Brodie Castle), there can be no dubiety about the significance of the superbly carved Celtic cross on the reverse side. Within the ruins of Elgin Cathedral there is a weathered granite stone. On one side the carvings include a huntsman with hawk and hounds; on the other there is a cross and four figures who, it is thought, are the four Evangelists. Neither stone is in its original site, the Elgin one being found in the vicinity of the parish kirk of St Giles. It is probably no coincidence that a number of Pictish stones have been found at or close to early centres of Christian worship. It would seem, therefore, that early churchmen deliberately picked out places that were already of some religious, or maybe even secular, significance. On Speyside, for instance, there are four early symbol stones set into the south wall of the parish kirk of Inveravon. Mortlach, too, has some stones as has Knockando, although the latter may not be such an ancient site. Also on Speyside, at the auld kirk of Arndilly near Craigellachie, there was another stone with 'rude figures carved on it'. Although erroneously describing it as a Druidical memorial, the Rev L. W. Forbes,

Side view of Sueno's Stone near Forres. Notice the vine-scroll and the strange-looking figures. Since this photograph was taken, the surrounds have been landscaped and the monument enclosed in a protective glass pavilion. (Photograph: the author)

writing in 1834, noted that there were resemblances between this stone, which by this time had been flitted to Arndilly House and one at Inveravon. It was possible, he considered, 'that our forefathers fixed their Christian temples on the sites of Druidical worship.'

The most remarkable of all the carved stones is Sueno's Stone at Forres not far from Burghead. This magnificent tall slab (inappropriately named it should be said) has on one face an Irish style ring-headed cross and on the other a battle scene and its aftermath of revenge and massacre. There are rows and rows of tiny figures, some engaged in battle, some running away, and some headless corpses — presumably prisoners who had been executed. Also depicted is the executioner — holding a severed head. One hypothesis is that this spectacular monument commemorates the defeat of the Picts by Kenneth MacAlpin. Others suggest that it marks a Scoto-Pictish triumph over the Norse. Whoever the combatants were, this extraordinary carved stone reveals, as Ian Shepherd has so aptly put it, 'war reporting on a monumentally self-confident scale.'

Another Scottish Dark Age treasure is the brecbennach of St Columba. While this beautifully ornamented portable shrine was later associated with Monymusk, and thus is called the Monymusk Reliquary, it was earlier held at Forglen in Banffshire. It is perhaps no coincidence that the kirk of Forglen was dedicated to Adamnan, the biographer of Columba. Although the shrine, which dates back to circa 700 AD, is of an Irish type, experts say that the animal decoration on it shows a distinctly Pictish influence. As one of the historic symbols of the Scottish nation, the reliquary, which held some potent relic of St Columba, would have been carried in religious processions and also used as a battle emblem. Indeed it is likely that it was employed for this purpose at the battle of Bannockburn.

Associated with an early Christian monastery at Deer in Buchan, is a Dark Age holy man — Drostan — who bears a Pictish name. Judging by dedications and local fairs that commemorated his name, his character and deeds made him a popular figure in the north-east. St Drostan fairs were celebrated not only at Old Deer but also at Rothiemay and Charlestown of Aberlour.

St Mary's Well, Orton, on Speyside. This holy well has a long history as a place of pilgrimage despite the Kirk's disapprobation. (Photograph: the author)

Near the ruined St Drostan's kirk at Aberlour is a well dedicated to the saint. It is situated in the grounds of the Aberlour-Glenlivet Distillery. There is no indication as to whether the spiritual quality of either the whisky or the water is enhanced or diluted thereby. Other early saints also had their names attached to sacred springs, wells and other places which were commonly believed to possess curative and other magical properties. It is probable that such beliefs pre-date the coming of Christianity. In taking over and developing for their own purposes wells and sites that had been objects of pagan veneration, the early churchmen showed good tactical sense.

Among the saints' wells with a long history of usage is St Fumac's at Drummuir in Strathisla north-west of Keith. In the old Botriphnie parish kirk there used to be a wooden statue of St Fumac. On the saint's day (the 3rd of May) the statue was taken from the kirk to the nearby holy well where it was washed before being carried in procession round the parish. When I visited the kirk in 1989, some children who were playing in the area kindly showed me to the well. In response to my enquiry as to whether it was still used, one boy said yes and proceeded to tell me that 'somebody had been crucified there a few months ago.' I think, nay strongly hope, that the word he meant to use was christened. Another Banffshire healing spring is Fergan's Well, which commemorates St Fergus another of the north's favourite holy men. This well, which is located on the steep slopes of Cnoc Fergan in Strathavon, was popular with those who were afflicted with skin diseases and running sores. The water was used both for washing the afflicted parts and for drinking — hopefully not in that order. But you had to pick your time for a visit, since the virtue of the water was greatly diminished after the month of September. The popular days for going to the well were the first Sunday in May and Easter Sunday. It was usual, too, to take a bottle of the spring water home for future use. A visitor to the well, writing in 1881, spoke to a local lad who had filled two bottles for taking away. The boy may have been a bit sceptical about the worth of the water as he assured his interrogator that it was not the 'real Glenlivet.'

Such beliefs were not confined to holy springs and pools. The granite tor of Clach-na-Bhan (the women's stone) high up on Ben Avon in the Eastern Cairngorms was considered to have magical properties. Pregnant women used to travel long distances to be 'chaired' in an armchair-shaped cavity in this huge and weathered lump of granite. Incredible as it may seem to us, since the rock is at an altitude of nearly 3,000 feet, the purpose of these pilgrimages was to ensure a safe pregnancy. Contact with the stone itself seems to have been important as single women also made use of it to secure a husband. An eye-witness account of a group pilgrimage to this magical rock formation is to be found in a 'New History of Aberdeenshire' (1875). The author witnessed in 1836 'the chairing of twelve full-bodied women, who had that morning come from Speyside, over twenty miles, to undergo the operation.' It is to be hoped that they used vehicles or ponies for at least part of their journey. Tradition, derived from ancient Gaelic mythology, tells us too that the lady of Fingal used to bathe in the rain-filled granite potholes. By the mid-nineteenth century these legends were being taken less seriously. An Invernessshire solicitor and clerk of the peace, writing anonymously, described being part of a 'jovial company' who mixed Athole Brose in one of the cavities and then drank toasts to the Ossianic heroes. When I visited Clach-na-Bhan on a hill-walking expedition, having nothing stronger to hand, I sampled the water from a pothole, taking it on trust that no 'full-bodied' woman, or anyone else for that matter, had been sitting in it lately.

The basis for beliefs and traditions that survived post-Reformation Calvinist disapproval was largely destroyed by 19th and 20th century rationalism and scepticism. However, one Moray community carries on an ancient Yule fire-festival. This is Burghead and the festival is the Burning of the Clavie — the Clavie, in this case, being constructed from whisky barrels and other combustible materials. Since it is unlucky to purchase any of their requirements, the participants rely on donated materials. On the evening of the 11th of January the Clavie is set alight — a burning peat is employed for this — and carried through the streets of the old part of the town. To be appointed Clavie King or leader of the Clavie crew is a high honour in Burghead. The crew who take it in turn to carry the blazing Clavie are all male and the office is hereditary. A stumble portends ill fortune. An extra bright blaze foretells specially good fortune in the year to come. To keep the fire going, the bearers feed in staves and a mixture of creosote and tar. Stopping at various places to change bearers and to refuel the barrel, the crew distribute smouldering faggots as good luck symbols and these are greatly prized by the 'Brochers', as locals are termed. Even the choice of date bears its own significance, as the 11th of January is the last day of the year by the old-style calendar — a form of reckoning that was abolished by government decree in 1752. In that year the calendar was reformed, with eleven days removed from the month of September. Many Scots resented the change and carried on with the old style of calendar, adding on the 'eleven lost days'.

We can't be absolutely certain how far back this or any other fire-festival goes. But the seamen of Burghead and other ports of Moray were condemned by 17th-century clerics because on the last day of December they 'superstitiously carried fyrr torches about their boats'. To ensure good luck, they took the torches and made a circuit of the boats. Fires of propitiation and purification were indeed widespread and, of course, held at other significant times of the year. The Beltane bonfires in May and their midsummer and Halloween equivalents also met frequent, although not universal, condemnation. Lachlan Shaw, the 18th-century historian of Moray, described the fire-festivals which he had witnessed as a lad. At midsummer eve, in lowland Moray farmers went 'about their fields of corn with burning torches in their hands, to obtain a blessing on their corns'. Interestingly, this presumably age-old ritual was conducted in deasil fashion — i.e. the participants went sunwise round the fields. As it was vital also to preserve their livestock, it was common practice, during the various fire-festivals, to make a sacrificial offer of food and to 'make the deasil'. How and when these rituals originated we cannot say, but they are surely ancient and were certainly once purposeful. These were ceremonies of great symbolic importance. We can say with more assurance roughly when and why these rituals came to be terminated. Although not all kirk sessions were condemnatory (presumably because their members knew the weight of public opinion), the Kirk as a whole disapproved. At Inveravon in 1714 the session condemned those who carried clavies through the fields and byres. It was an idolatrous offence, the parishioners were warned, to ascribe 'that power to the fire of sanctifieing your corn and cattle which is only proper and peculiar to the true and living God.' Alternative beliefs and rituals were not so easily disposed of, however, and, as late as 1774, the minister of Deskford cast scorn on 'the more ignorant and weak part of the parish' for burning of fires.

Fortunately, the solid, sensible folk of Burghead maintained their traditions. If we were able to bring them back, it would be nice to think that the present observance at Burghead, if not perhaps the contemporary rationale, would meet with the approval of our far distant ancestors. It is fitting indeed that this ancient rite is perpetuated at the former Pictish stronghold of Burghead. Appropriately, too, the final destination of the Clavie is on the Doorie Hill on the ramparts of the Pictish fort.

CHAPTER 2

Dark Age and Medieval Moray

'The treacherous nation of Moray'

In the middle of the 9th century the Kingdom of the Picts came to an end and the Gaelic-speaking Scots became the dominant force in the north-east. New territorial names appear. The region previously identified, either in whole or part, by the Pictish name of Fidach became known as Moray and its ruler as mormaer (probably originally a Pictish title). Although mormaers generally ranked with earls, in Moray the mormaers had extra-special authority and indeed ruled a very extensive province extending from east of the Spey to Knoydart and Glenelg in the west. For successive Scottish kings this was frontier territory and they faced challenge after challenge from the semi-independent rulers of Moray, who in their turn were threatened by the powerful earls of Orkney.

The north-east proved to be a battle-ground and an unlucky one for the Scottish royal house over a long period of time. In 954 the men of Moray killed Malcolm I. It was the Vikings, however, who slew his successor, Indulf, possibly at Cullen, eight years later. When in 966 King Dubh was killed at Forres, the 'men of Moray' were labelled by an unfriendly chronicler as 'the treacherous nation of Moray'. In the 11th century yet another Scottish ruler met an untimely end in the province, when Macbeth triumphed over Duncan I at a battle fought in 1040 at Pitgaveney near Elgin. The victor in this dynastic struggle was Mormaer of Moray. Duncan, the defeated king, was not the greybeard portrayed by Shakespeare in his play 'Macbeth'. In reality, he was a young man, and to spoil the story even more, he was slain not in his sleep but on the battlefield.

Unfortunately, while Shakespeare's tragedy is great drama, it is not very good history. Its perennial success as a play has, however, made Macbeth the best known of our early kings — and also the most maligned. There were, for example, no witches and therefore there is, despite the indefatigable efforts of some local antiquarians, no 'blasted heath' to show to tourists. In one respect, however, Shakespeare was reasonably accurate: he identified Macbeth with the north-east. It was his position as Mormaer of Moray that gave Macbeth his source of power and helped to ensure that he survived for 17 years. The fact, too, that he even risked leaving Scotland for a lengthy visit to Rome is some indication of the authority he commanded. When around 1050 Macbeth arrived in the Holy City, the pilgrim-king, according to an Irish chronicler, scattered charity to the poor 'like seed'. As ruler, too, Macbeth was astute enough to import Norman mercenaries to reinforce his army. It was not enough, however, as in 1054 Macbeth's levies were defeated by Earl Siward of Northumbria and Duncan's son, the future Malcolm III. Nevertheless, he held out in his northern stronghold for another three years until Malcolm Canmore triumphed again, defeating and killing Macbeth at Lumphanan. Even then, his northern henchmen refused to acknowledge Malcolm Canmore as their rightful king. They maintained the struggle, choosing Macbeth's stepson, Lulach, as his successor. King Lulach's reign was brief, however, as in 1058 he too was killed — slain like his stepfather in Aberdeenshire.

While Malcolm may have gained the crown, Macbeth's successors still contended for the throne. Brief though his reign may have been, Lulach's descendants and other claimants continued the struggle, posing problems for even such powerful monarchs as David I and William the Lion. By suppressing the earldom and annexing his opponents' lands, David I (reigned 1124–1153) undermined the basis for northern resistance. The former Celtic landowners were replaced by Anglo-Normans and other incomers whose loyalties were to the king, their feudal overlord. In the Laigh of Moray a Fleming, Freskin by name, was granted Duffus and other lands by David I. In time the Freskins so increased their holdings and power that they adopted the surname of De Moravia (which means of Moray). A fellow countryman, Berowald the Fleming, was given a fiefdom in 'the province of Moray' by Malcolm IV. In return for his fief — the lands of Innes and Nether Urquhart — he did military service in the king's castle at Elgin. The Comyns were yet another incoming family who exercised great power in the north. When William Comyn married a Scottish

Cantraydoune motte in Strathnairn. (Photograph: the author)

heiress, he succeeded also to his Celtic father-in-law's title of
Earl of Buchan and thus became the first of the new settler
families to acquire an earldom. Another branch of the Comyn
family became lords of Badenoch and thus controlled much of
Strathspey. Lochindorb Castle, built by John Comyn the Red,
was one of their strongholds.

While the 13th-century Lochindorb Castle is a stone-built
castle of enclosure, earlier Norman-style fortifications were
constructed of timber. Although the wooden castle buildings
have long disappeared, the earthen mounds or mottes, on
which they were built, very often survive as, for example, the
so-called Knight's Hillock which is just to the east of Innes
House. This artificial mound stands on the lands that long ago
were feued to Berewald the Fleming. Another fine motte can
be seen on the east side of the River Nairn at Cantraydoune.
(Dun — pronounced as doon — is Gaelic for a fort.) Situated
south-west of Cawdor Castle, which incidentally long post-dates
the Macbeth era, we can be fairly sure that this prominent motte
(10.5 metres high and 18 metres in diameter) is a relic from
the age of dynastic conflict and of the subsequent 'plantation'
of Moray. Significantly, the lands of Cantray were held by the

Scoto-Flemish Freskyn family who also built Duffus Castle near Elgin. Duffus is a splendid example of a mid-12th century motte and bailey castle. This keyhole-shaped fortification illustrates how the site was adapted, not always successfully, to fit new needs and new styles of construction. In the 13th century the wooden fence that protected the bailey or outer courtyard was replaced by a stone curtain wall, and the earthen mound was topped by a new stone keep. This, however, proved to be an engineering error, as the manmade motte couldn't bear the weight. A large chunk of the tower broke off and slipped down the bank. The block of masonry is still there, a silent rebuke to the builder's miscalculation.

In addition to Lochindorb, the Comyns had a stronghold at Dufftown. Strategically sited so as to command important lines of communication, Balvenie Castle dates back to the late 13th century, the heyday of Comyn power and prestige. Although rebuilt and altered by later proprietors, the great curtain wall and huge ditch demonstrate the military imperatives of what was then the most powerful family in the kingdom. To defend their interests in Strathspey the Comyns had another fortress at Kingussie. That castle no longer exists, but the Jacobite era fortified barracks erected on the site still survive.

While it was great barons who built, with royal approval, the like of Duffus and Balvenie, successive kings asserted their authority in more direct fashion by constructing castles in certain key locations. Royal castles were erected at Inverness, Auldearn, Forres, Elgin (where Berewald performed his knight-service) and maybe also at Cullen and Banff. Later demolition removed most of the traces of these erstwhile royal strongholds. Some of the sites as at Inverness and Elgin are clearly evident — on the Castlehill and Ladyhill respectively. Auldearn disappeared from the record after its seizure by Donald Macwilliam. It was replaced by a new edifice at Nairn of which nothing now remains. Although the evidence for it actually being a royal castle is absent, it is a strong probability that the one at Banff came into that category. At any rate more of the building survives than at other better documented sites. Substantial sections of a once massive outer wall, a postern gate, and part of the moat can still be seen. While little remains of the royal keeps of Banff, Moray and Nairn, Kildrummy in

Aberdeenshire is a splendid example of a 13th-century royal castle. This great curtain-walled fortress seemingly designed by Gilbert, Bishop of Caithness, for Alexander II was evidently designed to block and help control troublemakers from Moray. Gilbert, who died in 1245 and was the last pre-Reformation Scottish saint, would have been interested in the wellbeing of the neighbouring province, since he belonged to the De Moravia family.

The creation of royal burghs was also deliberate policy. In the 12th century successive monarchs founded burghs on their own lands. Thus burghs came into being at Auldearn, Forres, Elgin and Banff. However, the royal castle and nascent burgh at Auldearn were replaced in the time of William I by Nairn, which being at the mouth of the river of the same name was presumably regarded as a better site.

Forres retains to a remarkable degree its original medieval layout. Sited for practical reasons on the line of the direct road that links Inverness to other settlements in the fertile north-east lowlands, the main street, as with other comparable burghs, formed part of the King's highway — thus, of course, the name of High Street. Towards the centre of the town, the highway was left deliberately wide to accommodate the market. The market-cross and the tolbooth — which constituted the administrative headquarters of the burgh — were both located in this commercial hub. While the originals have gone, their Victorian replacements help us to appreciate the commercial logic behind the choice of site.

The parish kirk was another of the key structures of medieval Forres. The present Gothic revival-style St Laurence's church is also on the same site as the medieval kirk. At the west end stood the royal castle. Now only a green mound, capped by a Victorian obelisk, and the name Castle Hill mark the spot. Both burgh and castle were strategically situated — close to fords or bridging-points on the Mosset Burn and, further west, on the more difficult River Findhorn. Further protection for old Forres would have been provided by earth-works, later replaced by dykes, which enclosed the burgh. Present-day North Road and, on the other side of the High Street, Orchard Road and South Street mark the parameters of the old burgh. Running from the back dykes to the High Street were the tenements

The 12th century Birnie kirk was built on an old Celtic site. (Photograph: the author)

(originally not buildings but narrow plots of land) where the burgesses had their gardens and their dwellings. Originally all the houses, as some still do, stood gable on to the High Street. The wynds and closes, which gave access to the street, are a notable feature of the old-time burgh of Forres.

Eleven miles away to the east, Elgin, another of the very early royal burghs, has many similar features, most notably the closes and lanes leading off from the High Street and also the bulge in the town centre that served as the market-place. As at Forres, its fortifications have gone, but the medieval castle mound — Lady Hill — is physical evidence for the far-reaching changes that were wrought by the early medieval monarchs. As part of their policies of 'pacification' and settlement, the kings and their placemen introduced new men into the burghs. The settlers who, created the early burghs included Flemings and other immigrants from the continent and, in addition, southerners who spoke 'Inglis'. In time, this minority language, the tongue of a small but increasingly influential segment of society, replaced Gaelic as the language of the north-east lowlands and eventually, too, of the highlands of Banff, Moray and Nairn.

The new ideas that gained strength in Scotland from the 11th century onward were reflected in ecclesiastical design and architecture. Although the parish kirk of Birnie near Elgin is small and uncomplicated, its rounded arches well demonstrate the principles of the Romanesque or 'Norman' style of building. While the church, which was an early seat of the Bishop of Moray, also has a Norman font, its possession of the historic Ronnel Bell shows that relics of the old Celtic Church were not altogether discarded. Celtic saints were still venerated, as kirk dedications and place-names indicate. In Banffshire, for example, St Marnock is commemorated at Marnoch; in Moray, St Bridget or St Bride at Lhanbryde (the church of Bride); and in Nairnshire, St Adamnan at Barevan Kirk near Cawdor.

Administrative systems were, however, reorganised with parishs delimited and bishops appointed to supervise the parish clergy. Assuming that the tradition for Mortlach being a bishop's seat for the early Celtic Church is spurious, the first bishops in Moravia were royal appointees who, as well as extending the influence of the Roman Church, were also important feudal magnates. Birnie, Kinnedar (by Lossiemouth) and Spynie served, successively, as administrative centres for the diocese until Bishop Bricius Douglas applied for papal permission to move his cathedral from Spynie to the Kirk of the Holy Trinity 'juxta Elgyn'. This did not take effect until 1224 when his De Moravian successor, Bishop Andrew, had taken office. It was another De Moravian bishop, the saintly Gilbert of Caithness who performed the service of consecration. Thanks to the generosity of his powerful relatives and, to an even greater extent, King Alexander II, the cathedral when eventually completed was the finest building of its type in Scotland.

Interestingly, Alexander II (reigned 1214–1249) also paid for a chaplain to say masses within the cathedral for the soul of his ancestor, King Duncan. Was he cocking a snoot at the long dead 'usurper' Macbeth and the later Moray-based claimants, who had threatened the Canmore dynasty over such a long period of time? In addition to foundations for the Blackfriars and the

In 1948 Benedictine monks returned to Pluscarden Abbey which had been abandoned after the Reformation. (Photograph: the author)

Greyfriars in the town of Elgin, King Alexander, a frequent visitor to Moray, established in 1230 a priory at Pluscarden. Originally a Valiscaulian monastery (like Beauly), Pluscarden became part of the much more influential Benedictine Order in 1454. Abandoned after the Reformation, the Benedictines returned after the Second World War and started the process of restoration. Now the work is well advanced and the 'new' Pluscarden Abbey with its magnificent stained glass windows is a fascinating place to visit. At least there was something to restore at Pluscarden, unlike the even older Priory of Urquhart which has vanished altogether. Founded in the early 12th century by David I, it was also a Benedictine house but was united to Pluscarden when that monastery was transferred to the Benedictines.

David I — 'the sair sanct for the croon' — also founded Kinloss Priory (1150). Regrettably very little remains of this once prosperous Cistercian monastery. Its stones were quarried for secular purposes and part of the grounds employed as a graveyard. As it is close to the important RAF Kinloss Airbase it serves too as a wargraves cemetery. In this quiet spot where monks once pursued their peaceful avocations, there are rows of uniform grey stones. Erected by the Commonwealth War Graves Commission, these trim stones bear the names of young airmen from different countries who were killed or died during the Second World War. Quite a few gravestones commemorate more recent but equally tragic training accidents.

While our 20th century civilisation has transformed this former monastic refuge, the monks of the medieval world were well acquainted with the effects of war. The Cistercian monks may have tried to shut themselves away from the world, but the world willy-nilly sometimes came to them as in 1303 when Edward I brought a huge army to Kinloss. For 10 days the all-powerful King of England stayed at the abbey, with his knights and men-at-arms camped nearby.

Edward I had been north before, however, when in 1296 he began his campaign to subjugate Scotland. After humbling his erstwhile puppet, John Balliol, and forcing his surrender at Montrose, the English king continued his northward march. Taking Aberdeen he then headed for Elgin, camping on successive nights at Kintore, Fyvie, Banff, Cullen and then in the Enzie on the east side of the Spey. After fording the Spey, Elgin 'a good castle and a good town' was occupied. While at Elgin the 'Hammer of the Scots' received the submission of the leading men of the area. Sending punitive forces into Badenoch and other mountainous areas, he then proceeded south following the Spey to Rothes. The contemporary diarist to whom we are indebted for this information then tells us that he took his main army over the Cabrach to Kildrummy in Aberdeenshire. The diarist was unimpressed with Innerquharanche, the stopping place in the Cabrach, 'where there was no more than 3 houses in a row between two mountains.'

Although Edward had left garrisons in key fortresses in this seemingly conquered country, English rule was unpopular and in 1297 the Scots rebelled. In the south the risings were led by William Wallace and in the north by Andrew de Moray. Duffus, Forres, and Elgin were among the castles retaken. Moray and Wallace combined forces and won a considerable victory at Stirling Bridge, but Moray unfortunately died soon after probably as a result of battle wounds. In the following year, 1298, Wallace lost to Edward at Falkirk. The resistance movement continued, however, forcing Edward to raise another immense and irresistible army. Sweeping away again all who stood in his way, he invaded Scotland in 1303, once again making Moray his ultimate target just as he had done in 1296 and, for that matter, like the Romans too in their day. On this occasion it was Kinloss, as we have seen, that was his turning point. Seizing Lochindorb, Edward made this Comyn stronghold his base for a month while he consolidated his position in the strategically very important north-east.

Then in 1306 Robert the Bruce took up arms against Edward and resumed the struggle for Scotland's independence. Unfortunately for him, by slaying his rival the Red Comyn (the Lord of Badenoch) in a quarrel, Bruce thereby ensured that henceforward the Comyns were his deadly enemies. John Comyn, Earl of Buchan (the Black Comyn) opposed Bruce, although his wife the Countess of Buchan had crowned Bruce at Scone and consequently was afterwards imprisoned in England. David, Bishop of Moray, who was an uncle of Andrew de Moray, was another staunch patriot — one of the many Moray men who strove and fought to free their country.

In 1307 and 1308 Bruce fought a campaign in the north-east that was partly a war against the English garrisons who held the royal castles and partly a civil war against the Comyns who still upheld the cause of John Balliol. Robert I defeated the Comyns at battles fought near Huntly and Inverurie and then commenced on the notorious harrying of Buchan. After destroying the Comyn fortresses in Aberdeenshire in 1308, Bruce controlled most of the north-east, the last castle to fall being Banff which was taken in 1310.

As the Scots surged towards eventual triumph, Robert I punished his enemies, taking their lands and rewarding his friends. One who profited was his nephew and lieutenant, Thomas Randolph, who in 1312 was created Earl of Moray. One of Randolph's most spectacular feats was the recapture of Edinburgh Castle. The new Earl played his part in the Scottish victory at Bannockburn in 1314, and on the death of Bruce in 1329 was made Guardian of Scotland. Darnaway near Forres was the Earl's seat although the so-called, but indeed spectacular, Earl Randolph's Hall was probably built in the 15th century.

Bruce's policy of rewards and punishment caused trouble for his child successor, David II. The sons of the nobles who had lost their estates sought revenge and in the 1330s Balliols and Comyns, with military support from Edward III of England, came close to the success that had eluded their predecessors. Like his grandfather Edward III was able to deploy a massive and irresistible army. In 1336 he marched north and wasted the lands of Moray. But permanent conquest was not so easily attained, as David II's supporters maintained a dogged resistance. Seen in retrospect, the tide had begun to turn in the previous year — in 1335. Once again it was a Sir Andrew de Moray, the son of Wallace's comrade-in-arms, who dictated the course of events. In 1335 at Culblean (between Ballater and Aboyne) Moray's generalship gave the patriots a morale-boosting victory over the supporters of Edward Balliol who, like his father the former King John, played the part of English puppet.

It had been the policy of Robert I to destroy most of the former royal castles to deny them to the enemy. The rebuilding of some of these fortresses and the construction of others in the late 14th and 15th centuries were signs that this was a time of political uncertainty and of civil discord. Lochindorb, for instance, was strengthened as one of the strongholds of Alexander Stewart, Lord of Badenoch, a son of Robert II. Through marriage, Alexander Stewart gained the title of Earl of Buchan in 1382 but he was better known as the Wolf of Badenoch. (The name was derived from the wolf that adorned his heraldic crest.) Although appointed king's justiciar (or lieutenant) for the north, Alexander Stewart was a troublemaker on a grand scale. He terrorised the country and, struggling for supreme power, clashed with the Earl of Moray. The other Scottish magnates were so appalled by his conduct that in 1388 they secured his dismissal from the post of justiciar on the grounds that he was 'useless to the community'. But the Wolf was not tamed. When in 1389 he was condemned by the Bishop of Moray for deserting his wife, he hit back by seizing the Bishop's lands in Badenoch. The Bishop's retaliation was to excommunicate his troublesome foe. But then the Wolf of Badenoch inflicted a terrible revenge. In 1390 he swooped into lowland Moray and put the burghs of Forres and Elgin to the flames. Sadly, not even Elgin cathedral was spared. The Wolf's 'wild and wicked Highlandmen' set fire to this truly magnificent edifice, the 'Lantern of the North'. The Wolf's caterans destroyed, as a chronicler lamented, 'the noble and highly adorned church of Moray, the delight of the country and ornament of the kingdom, with all the books, charters, and other goods of the country placed therein.' Although Robert III did eventually manage to force him to submit and to seek absolution, the Wolf remained a powerful figure till his death in 1405. But in abusing his authority and position, the Wolf of Badenoch engendered insecurity and destroyed social stability in what till then had been a tolerably settled society. For a long time thereafter Moray and the neighbouring counties were plagued by feuding lairds and cattle-thieving caterans.

Ironically, after the demise of the Wolf of Badenoch, a degree of order was enforced by his gifted, bastard son, who was also Alexander Stewart. After gaining, by unscrupulous means, lands in Aberdeenshire and the title of Earl of Mar by marriage, this brigand-turned-law-enforcer maintained a measure of law and order. As Earl of Mar, he faced in 1411 a massive invading Highland army led by Donald, Lord of the Isles. Donald's army had marched through Moray and Banff, causing panic among the douce folk of Forres and Elgin and the other settled communities of the north-east. Although the battle fought near Inverurie was inconclusive, the Highlanders retreated. This bloody conflict fought on the 'sair' field of Harlaw was long remembered, however, becoming enshrined in folksong and legend.

When people fear for their lives and property, they look to their defences. Judging by the number of medieval keeps and towers that even yet survive, the great magnates and other lairds of late medieval Moray saw strong walls as a military and political necessity. There was building and rebuilding at many significant sites including Auchindoun and Balvenie on Speyside. In the same district can be seen, too, the massive remnants of Drumin Castle. Built where the rivers Livet and Avon meet, Drumin was once, it is said, a stronghold of the Wolf of Badenoch. Spectacular, too, in a different way are the

shattered cliff-top towers of Findlater Castle. This crag-clinging
Ogilvie fortress is perched on the sea cliffs between Sandend
and Cullen. Worth seeing, too, is Spynie Palace, the massively
impressive seat of the Bishops of Moray. A great deal of work
has gone into the restoration of this formidable palace-fortress,
which is located midway between Elgin and Lossiemouth.
Located close to Loch Spynie, it was strategically located as
the loch was once much larger and was indeed an inlet of
the sea. Much of the land round Spynie, it should be said,
was reclaimed when the loch was drained in the 19th century.
Although now separate from the loch, the Palace was on a
prime defensive site on a spit of land projecting into the loch.
There was once too a harbour by the palace and indeed a
burgh of Spynie. This formerly active seaport, however, died
when the inlet became blocked. Although little remains of the
nearby old kirk, it is worth recalling that Spynie was until 1224
the bishop's seat. (The grave of Ramsay Macdonald, Britain's
first Labour Prime Minister is located in the kirkyard. Visitors,
though, should note that the 'new' Spynie Kirk is several miles
to the west. It is an 18th-century building and interesting in its
own right.)

The surviving buildings of Spynie Palace are awesomely
impressive and belong largely to the 15th century. This was
an age, of course, when bishops possessed secular power no less
than their spiritual. In the early 15th century Bishop Innes, a
near contemporary of the Wolf of Badenoch, built an imposing
defensive gatehouse. The threat posed by unscrupulous feudal
lords drove the bishops into further construction. In the mid-
15th century the Gordons posed the major threat. Tradition has
it that, when the first Earl of Huntly was excommunicated by
Bishop David Stewart, the noble earl responded by threatening
to pull the bishop 'out of his pigeon-hole'. Bishop David,
accordingly, strengthened his 'pigeon-house' by building an
immense fortification. This is the six storey-high 'Davy's Tower'
which was one of the largest and grandest of the Scottish
tower-houses.

If not at that time, then certainly later (as later chapters will
show) the Gordon clan, despite the possession by the earls of
substantial territories in the county, were both feared and hated
by the good folk of Moray. According to a traditional saying —

'The Gordon, the gool (the corn marigold), and the hoodie-craw
Were the three worst ills that Moray e'er saw.'

'Davy's Tower' at Spynie Palace. This former residence of the Bishops
of Moray is not at present (1992) open to the public. (Photograph: the
author)

CHAPTER 3

Religious Zeal and Civil Strife

To view the shattered fragments of Kinloss Abbey, it is difficult to imagine that these ruins were once the heart of a thriving community. The laybrothers who served the Cistercian monks tilled land that was renowned for its fertility. In the 16th century the cultivation of fruit-trees was one of the Kinloss specialities, the monks being aided by an expert gardener brought from France by Abbot Robert Reid. Reid, who became administrative head of the abbey in 1526, was extremely able and so was promoted to other important posts, serving both Church and State. While at Kinloss, however, he improved the library and employed a celebrated artist to paint new altar-pieces for the three chapels in the abbey kirk.

Monasticism, however, had by then lost its former vigour. Even as far back as 1454 Urquhart had been united to Pluscarden because of declining numbers. Around 1535 the Abbot of Kinloss started to sell off the lands of Strathisla to sitting tenants. Wealthy laymen too, when making endowments, were bypassing the monasteries, some preferring to create new-style collegiate churches. The parish kirk of Cullen is a good example of this kind of church. In 1543 some pious lairds and other leading figures set up a small religious community who would care for the spiritual needs of the populace and, above all, say masses for the souls of the founders. The endowments at Cullen were sufficiently generous to pay for a Provost and no fewer than six other resident clergymen plus two choirboys. One of the treasures of the present-day kirk is the magnificently-carved monument which commemorates the principal benefactor — Alexander Ogilvie of Findlater who died in 1554.

Cullen also has another interesting decorative feature. This is a stone cupboard which in pre-Reformation days was used for storing the consecrated bread and wine that were used in services. As with a similar aumbry or sacrament house at the ruined old kirk at nearby Deskford, there are two angels

The simple exterior of the Auld Kirk of Cullen belies the interest of its interior which contains several intriguing monuments. There are many interesting stones in the kirkyard as well. (Photograph: the author)

carved in stone above the recess. They are depicted as holding a monstrance, an ornamental vessel which was used for displaying the consecrated wafer. As an inscription at Deskford indicates, the donors 'of this present lovable work of sacrament house' were the afore-said Alexander Ogilvie and his wife Elizabeth Gordon. The fact that many of the powerful Banffshire lairds were agin the Reformation helps to explain why such 'idol-atrous' features survived the ecclesiastical despoilers of the 16th and 17th centuries. Another aumbry at Pluscarden had evidently been damaged and is not in its original state. Three medieval crosses, however, survived in Moray — in the kirkyards at Dallas, Duffus, and Kinneddar. Although some of the neighbouring lairds were perfervid prebyterians, they survived probably because as mercat crosses they served a secular function. Since the church was the obvious meeting place for the folk of the parish, it was quite common for markets to be conducted in the kirkyard.

By the 16th century, however, many of the kirks were suffering from neglect, their teinds having been siphoned off to help maintain cathedrals, monasteries, and collegiate churches like Cullen. The emoluments of the Provost of the Collegiate Church of Cullen included 'the fruits of the vicarage of Rathven (at Buckie) ... together with the manse and glebe.' Not surprisingly the parish clergy lost status as well as income. But the wealth garnered for the benefit of cathedrals, monasteries and other religious houses engendered both envy and criticism. The Protestant reformers in Scotland echoed those English critics who decried cathedrals as 'dens of loitering lubbers'.

Too many of the abbots and bishops were noted for their worldliness rather than their spirituality. As great magnates in their own right, they were also frequently embroiled in secular disputes and family feuds. As the Wolf of Badenoch had done in his day, leading laymen pillaged church properties, as when in 1515 Lord Gordon, son of the Earl of Huntly, raided and plundered the Abbey of Kinloss. Pluralism was another abuse. That led to ecclesiastics acquiring great personal wealth by drawing revenues from several benefices. For instance, Andrew Forman, Bishop of Moray (1501–1514), was also Commendator (equivalent to Abbot) of no fewer than three different abbeys.

Nevertheless, when in the late 1550s the storm of the Reformation broke, there was little enthusiasm for change in Moray, Banff and Nairn. There were admittedly some violent outbreaks. In July 1559 the Carmelite friars in Banff were assailed and their house burned 'under sylens of nicht'. Nothing now remains of that friary, nor indeed of the Blackfriars' house at Elgin. The Franciscan kirk in Elgin also became ruinous when their community was dispersed. Interestingly, though, in the 19th century the former Greyfriars church was rebuilt and restored for use as a convent chapel.

Events in the south brought the old regime down when in 1560 the Protestant Lords of the Congregation, with considerable English assistance, defeated the Catholic party and their French allies. Even the return to Scotland in 1561 of the Catholic Mary, Queen of Scots, did not change the situation. Indeed Mary's decision to make her Protestant half-brother, Lord James Stewart, Earl of Moray strengthened the reforming cause in the north-east. This appointment, however, provoked a long-lasting feud with the extremely powerful, and staunchly Catholic, Gordon clan. Rather incredibly for a devotee of the auld religion, the Earl of Huntly, who led the Gordons, came out against the Queen. In 1562 Huntly's men were, however, defeated by Moray at Corrichie near Aberdeen. Mary was a spectator at the battle which brought about the defeat, and subsequent death through apoplexy, of her most powerful Catholic subject, the 4th Earl of Huntly, the erstwhile Cock of the North. The English ambassador graphically described the earl's sudden demise — 'withowte ether belowe or stroke . . . he sodenlie, fawlethe from his horse starke dedde . . .' Some of the rebels were executed, including one of Huntly's sons, Sir John Gordon. By refusing to surrender Findlater and Auchindoun castles, which he held at that time, Sir John had incurred the Queen's wrath and, therefore, received no mercy.

In this very uncertain situation, the first Protestant clergymen had to gang warily. Local tradition maintained that Gilbert Garden, minister at Fordyce, carried a sword when he entered the pulpit. With so many recalcitrant Catholic lairds in Banffshire, this may well have been a sensible precaution.

Another leading figure who played to form by putting his own and his family's interests first was Patrick Hepburn who was Bishop of Moray at the time of the Reformation. The Bishop had already disposed of most of the Church lands. Needless to say this grasping cleric and his many relatives were the chief beneficiaries. Initially Bishop Hepburn supported the revolutionaries until 'the rascal multitude' sacked the Abbey of Scone. This hurt his pocket, since as Commendator he had drawn a lucrative income from that monastery. Secure in his own stronghold at Spynie, he defied the Reformers until his death in 1573. The 4th Earl of Bothwell, whose relations with Mary, Queen of Scots, led to her downfall, was a nephew of the bishop. When Mary was forced to surrender at Carberry in 1567, Bothwell sought refuge at Spynie. Betrayed, though, by the Bishop's illegitimate sons, Bothwell had to cut and run. He escaped to Orkney and eventually to exile and imprisonment in Denmark.

While the Bishop looked after his own interests, his cathedral, deprived of income and function fell into neglect. It was no longer used as a bishop's seat and it was not required for parish use as the burgh already had its own St Giles kirk. When in 1567 the Privy Council was short of cash, it authorised the removal and sale of lead from the roof. Subsequent proposals to repair the damage were never implemented, so the buildings were allowed to decay.

While the great men contested for power, more humble folk had to abandon age-old beliefs and discard the habits of a lifetime — as, for example, when Isabel Umphray of Elgin was warned by the kirk session to keep away from the cathedral kirk. Since she was further instructed not to 'pray on her bairn's grave', it may be presumed that she had entered one of the chapels to pray for the soul of her dead child.

While the battle of Corrichie had been a humiliation, Gordon power was by no means broken and both the 5th and 6th earls played significant roles in state affairs. They carried on their old feuds, however, including that with the Morays. After the assassination in 1570 of the Earl of Moray, who was then Regent, the earldom was bestowed on another leading Protestant, James Stewart of Doune, son-in-law of the former Regent. A series of disputes intensified the long-standing rivalry between the 6th Earl of Huntly and the comely young Earl of Moray — the Bonnie Earl — who was apparently well regarded by the Queen. In 1592 the king, suspicious of Moray's loyalty, ordered his arrest and ill-advisedly gave the commission to his arch-rival, the Earl of Huntly. Huntly led a large party of retainers from Edinburgh to Moray's residence at Donibristle in Fife. When the Bonnie Earl refused to surrender, his house was put to the torch. Moray tried to escape but was overtaken and slain nearby. The lamentations of his family and of the Protestant faction generally are commemorated in the splendid ballad which concludes —

'Oh! lang will his lady
Look frae the Castle Doune
Ere she sees the Earle o Moray
Come sounding through the toon.

Since Huntly and other leading offenders were not punished very effectively, Lady Doune, the Bonnie Earl's mother sought vengeance. To put pressure on the king, she refused to bury her son's corpse, keeping it for six years until eventually the Privy Council compelled her to inter the remains. Lady Doune also commissioned a banner made from fine linen which depicts her son's corpse — slashed and bloody and punctured with bullets. Inset in one corner are the blazing buildings of Donibristle manor. On a scroll, emanating from the dead man's mouth, are the words 'God revenge my cause'. This banner, a memento of a mother's vengeful grief, still exists and can be seen in the Great Hall of Darnaway Castle. Darnaway, near Forres, is a building of considerable historic interest and is the principal residence of the present-day Moray family.

Eventually, too, the warring families were reconciled. Strange to relate, James the new Earl of Moray set the seal on the reconciliation by marrying Lady Anne Gordon, the daughter of the man who had slain his father. Two years after the murder of the Bonnie Earl, the 6th Earl of Huntly himself fell foul of the king. While Huntly did beat off a royal force under the Earl of Argyll at the battle of Glenlivet in 1594, this ineffectual counter-revolutionary was forced to submit and, nominally at least, to accept the new faith.

Some of the Ogilvies also upheld the old faith. Indeed John Ogilvie, a Banffshire-born Jesuit priest suffered martyrdom for propagating that faith. Condemned by an episcopalian court for denying royal supremacy over the Church, Ogilvie was hanged at Glasgow in 1615. Canonised in 1976, St John Ogilvy is Scotland's only post-Reformation saint. Father Ogilvie was connected to the Ogilvies of Keith. This family had a castle on the outskirts of Keith. But all that survives is the now ruinous Milton Tower.

The Catholics displayed similar intolerance. Where the Roman Catholics were dominant as in the parish of Rathven in Banffshire, they tried to browbeat the local Protestants. David Forrester, the zealous minister of the parish, complained in 1626 of the conduct of one of the local lairds, George Gordon of Farnauchtie. George Gordon had, at the conclusion of the church service, stood at the entrance and made a public proclamation, 'in the name and authority of the Marquis of Huntly', that none of his tenants 'suld frequent the hearing of the word on the Sabbath day at the Kirk of Rathven under

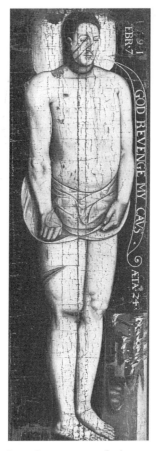

The banner displaying the corpse of the murdered Bonnie Earl of Moray can be seen at Darnaway Castle. (Photograph: National Galleries of Scotland — courtesy of the Earl of Moray)

pain of losing house and land, and under pain of incurring the wrath of the said Marquis, thair maister.'

When in the 1630s Charles I ran into difficulties, religious and political strife was resumed. Beginning with the signing of the National Covenant in 1638, the Scots carried through a religious and constitutional revolution. The Covenanters wanted to return to unalloyed presbyterianism and sought, therefore, to rid the Kirk of episcopalian rites and bishops (restored in a modified form by that canny monarch James VI). In the north-east, however, the Gordons, whose chief now bore the title of Marquis, remained loyal to the king. But the armies of the Covenant were too strong. The Covenanters seized Aberdeen, a loyalist stronghold, and then occupied Banff, burning the house of Sir George Ogilvie (later Lord Banff).

The Covenanters, though, had some strong supporters in Moray and Nairn — Alexander, the 15th Brodie of Brodie, for one. In 1640 this puritanical laird, along with the Laird of Innes and the parish minister of Elgin, entered Elgin Cathedral to destroy the richly painted rood screen. On one side of this wooden screen, which had survived many years of neglect, there was a painting of the crucifixion; on the other the day of judgement was depicted. But, although painted 'in excellent culloris', the rood screen was regarded as a Popish symbol and therefore had to be destroyed. But that was not the end of the affair. Some of the timber was carried to the minister's house to be used as firewood. To the folk of Elgin this seemed to be compounding the sacrilege. Tales were spread through the town that the timber from the cathedral wasn't burning as normal — that 'each night the fire went out . . . and could not be held in to kindle the morning fire as use is; whereat the servants and others marvelled and thereupon the minister left off and forebore to bring in or burn any more of that timber in his house.' That these stories received some credence shows perhaps a lack of public sympathy for such iconoclastic acts.

Alexander Brodie at least suffered retribution for his adherence to the Convenanting cause. In 1645 royalist troops, under the command of James Graham, the Marquis of Montrose, burned and plundered his castle. Brodie Castle, a tower-house of 1567, had defensive features but these offered but modest protection and were not strong enough to stop a determined assault. Following their spectacular victory at the battle of Inverlochy in February 1645, the Marquis of Montrose and his formidable Irish lieutenant Alasdair MacColla had invaded the north-east. Montrose, a brilliant leader, had been commissioned by Charles I to restore royal authority in Scotland. All men between the ages of 16 and 60 were charged to 'ryse and serve the king . . . under pane of fyre and suord.' Those

Elgin Cathedral from Cooper Park

Elgin Cathedral from the Cooper Park — an old view.

who refused were left to the not too tender mercies of this largely Highland and Irish force. In addition to Brodie, other leading Covenanters suffered loss and depredation when their mansions and other properties were raided and plundered.

Elgin was pillaged — this task being allocated to the Grants whose laird had joined Montrose. The leading Covenanters had, however, made themselves scarce, taking refuge at Spynie, which in those days was still a formidable fortress. Banff, too, was despoiled. Afterwards, the burgesses of Banff sent a plea to Parliament seeking compensation. They had suffered, they claimed, because of their 'zealous affection, adherence, and concurrence to the covenant. Our haill means,' they complained, 'both horses, nolt (cattle), cloaths, corn, and merchant guids . . . were all spolizit and awy taken be James Graham, and his most cruel, unnatural, and merciless associates, in the month of March 1645.' Graham of Montrose meantime had a burden of his own to bear. His fifteen-year-old son, who had endured the terrible hardships of a winter campaign, died at Fochabers and was buried nearby in Bellie kirkyard.

Back in Moray after a foray to the south, Montrose had reached Auldearn by the 8th of May, 1645. As before, the ruling classes of the North East were divided. Huntly had kept aloof but two of his sons were in Montrose's camp. The Brodies, the Roses of Kilravock and other local leaders were still strong for the Covenant. Calling out their retainers, Rose of Kilravock (a young man 'of a sweet and affable temper') and the other Covenanting lairds marched to Inverness and joined a Covenanting force led by Sir John Hurry.

Although he had a numerically superior army, Hurry attempted the difficult manoeuvre of a surprise attack. But this necessitated a night-march. Pouring rain during the march from Inverness, however, thwarted the Covenanters' hopes. Not only did the rain tire his men but it dampened the gunpowder in their muskets. While still some miles away from Auldearn, Hurry ordered his men to fire a volley to dry their guns. Unfortunately for him, a sudden change of wind carried the sound to Royalist scouts. This last minute warning enabled Alasdair MacColla to take a few hundred men out to face Hurry's onslaught. While MacColla's small force held up the Covenanters' attack, Montrose managed to muster and deploy the rest of his army. It was a prolonged and desperately fought struggle but, after recovering from their initial surprise, the Royalists eventually triumphed.

In recent years the accepted story of the battle of Auldearn has been revised by David Stevenson of Aberdeen University. He discards the old notion that Montrose implemented during the battle a previously conceived tactical bluff. The reality is that, since he was taken by surprise, Montrose's victory was achieved not by a mythical master-plan but rather by the ferocious courage of his men — Irish and Highlanders and Gordons from the shires of Aberdeen and Banff. Shock charges by Gordon cavalry turned the issue at crucial points in the battle. Montrose's men inflicted heavy casualties on their opponents. No quarter was given and many perished while trying to escape.

'And No Quarter' is the title of a historical novel written by Maurice Walsh. First published in 1937, the novel is based on Montrose's campaign of 1644–45. While his plot is fanciful, Walsh, a skilful storyteller, wrote an exciting yarn. In describing the battle of Auldearn, Walsh, followed the then accepted sequence of events and, an Irishman himself, gave the Irish side of the story. As he had been an exciseman in Moray for many years, Walsh knew the area well. Having a strong sense of place, he worked a number of local landmarks into the plot. These include Ardclach Bell-tower, Lochindorb castle, and Spynie Palace.

As for Montrose, Auldearn was followed by other triumphs but eventually his luck ran out. In September 1645 his depleted army was surprised and routed at Philiphaugh. Five years later James Graham, Marquis of Montrose, was hanged in Edinburgh. His royal master, Charles I, had been beheaded in London in the previous year, 1649.

Meantime, the Kirk had been disciplining those locals who had fought for the royalists. The offenders were summoned by the presbytery and obliged to seek forgiveness . . . for their part 'in the wicked rebellione'. Endeavouring to enforce religious conformity, the Puritans sought the removal or destruction of the surviving emblems of Popery. The Provincial Assembly decreed in 1649 that 'all the superstitious monuments' within the various churches be demolished. One monument that caused particular offence was 'that heart with arrows and crosess in Fordyce.'

Not long after the death of Montrose, the future Charles II landed at the mouth of the Spey. He was able to return from exile because the Covenanters, enraged at the English for executing their king, had sent commissioners (including Alexander Brodie) to offer him the crown of Scotland on condition that he signed the Covenant. Folk memory at Garmouth, where a plaque commemorates the landing of 1650, long preserved the name of 'King' Milne, the local man who carried the monarch ashore in pick-a-back style. The attempt to restore the Stewart fortunes was a failure and led to the Cromwellian occupation which lasted until 1660. In consequence, Alexander Brodie, who had been appointed a Lord of the Session, had to demit office. Lord Brodie, as he continued to be called, wrestled with his conscience but decided 'in the strength of the Lord to eschew and avoid employment under Cromwell.' His cousin, Brodie of Lethen, nevertheless, did not scruple from selling the stones from the Abbey of Kinloss for the construction of the Cromwellian citadel at Inverness. After Charles regained his British throne in 1660,

Lord Brodie went to London to seek recompense from the king for the loss sustained by himself and his friends during the years of civil strife. Uneasy about compromising his position (he had become, he confessed, 'a speckled bird'). Brodie gained an audience with the king. The date — the 13th of May 1662 — was inauspicious. His mission was a failure. The very next day he left London and departed for home.

Ironically visitors to Brodie Castle (it is now a National Trust property) can see a large portrait of Charles II. Although it may stretch credulity a bit, it was, according to family tradition, a gift from the Merry Monarch himself to that arch-Covenanter Alexander Brodie.

Although the return of Charles II meant that bishops were also restored, Lord Brodie and most of the other lairds of Moray and Nairn still favoured the Presbyterian form of church government. When Episcopalian clergymen were installed in the different parishes, some of the landed gentry, including various Brodies and Grants, absented themselves and were fined for non-attendance. The Roses of Kilravock in Nairnshire, like the Brodies, were a Covenanting and 'godly' family. As had been the case with Alexander Brodie, a pious wife, Margaret Innes, instilled Hugh, the 14th baron of Kilravock, with her faith and spiritual zeal and thus helped him to withstand governmental fines and threats. In 1673 a report to the Privy Council stated that 'seditious meitinges and conventicles' were being conducted in the shire of Elgin. Ousted Presbyterian clergymen from Ross, it was said, were holding conventicles. It was Charles, the 6th Earl of Moray, who was given the task of suppressing such illegal services. Lord Moray, a staunch royalist and later too a Jacobite, was a loyal servant to both Charles II and his successor, James VII. (Later, when serving as commissioner for James VII in Scotland, he announced his conversion to Roman Catholicism.) The Brodies and Roses remained on the other side of the religious and political divide, and some at least of the Covenanting preachers were given refuge and protection at Kilravock Castle.

There was, though, no refuge and protection for the poor, deluded creatures who were accused of witchcraft. For godly men of all denominations confessed witches were agents of the Devil and thus were a danger to society. Some accused witches were healers — the 'cunning' men and women — who existed in all communities. At Banff in 1631 John Philp admitted before Lord Deskford that at Fintray (in Aberdeenshire) he had used charms and spells to heal the sick. In confessing that he had invoked the aid of the Queen of the Fairies to cure a boy of the fever, he probably sealed his own fate. That he was also described as a vagabond did not help his case, as the central government had been clamping down on vagrants. The timing of his offences was also unlucky, since John Philp's trial coincided with an outbreak of witch mania. In consequence, there had been many executions, not just in Scotland but on the Continent as well. It is perhaps not too surprising, therefore, that this unfortunate man was sentenced to be burned as a warlock.

Widespread persecution on a European scale had begun with the medieval Church and was intensified by zealots, both Protestant and Catholic. In the 16th and 17th centuries there were periods when witch-hunting became in parts of Europe a veritable mania. 1644 was one of the peak years for persecution. It was also a time of political and military strife, which was lucky for two Rathven witches who escaped prosecution because the minister 'fearing danger' was unable to bring the kirk session together. Since they next appear in the record as 'fugitives to the hielands', this pair of suspects seem to have escaped the wrath of the session.

As happened elsewhere in Europe, foreign occupation brought some relief. During the period of the Cromwellian occupation, prosecutions in Scotland were halted for a time. This seeming leniency was resented, as when, in 1657, the minister of Cullen complained to the presbytery that a Margaret Philp had been released from custody. Although she had been apprehended for witchcraft, 'nevertheless, the civil power,' the minister lamented, 'delayed to administrat justice upon her . . . and she was set at libertie again . . .' That the evidence against her was ludicrous in the extreme did not seem to perturb the kirk luminaries of Banffshire. Margaret Philp had, it was alleged, confessed to feeding the devil (who had appeared in the form of a hare) and also, with several others had gone for a sail in a riddle. Although they could not proceed with civil proceedings, the presbytery could, and did, excommunicate this wretched woman. After the Restoration in 1660, there was an outburst of witch mania which resulted in the death of around 300 witches in Scotland between spring 1661 and autumn 1662. While many had confessed their guilt, their confessions had been induced by torture. What brought this particular outbreak to an end was the decision by the Privy Council to curb the use of torture.

Quite a few of the accused were probably deluded. Some must have been prone to fantasy. Where torture was applied, any kind of confession was, of course, possible. Undoubtedly, too, some of the victims of the witch-craze were pests and social nuisances. Prosecutions usually started after smallholders and other humble folk had complained of some act, or suspected act, of malevolent witchcraft. But, as Christine Larner pointed out in her superlative study 'Enemies of God', accusations of witchcraft would not have gone very far, if the educated elite had not shared these beliefs. In the age of witch mania, the foremost intellects in Scotland, and elsewhere in Europe, maintained that witchcraft threatened social stability.

In the diaries of Alexander, Lord Brodie, we see the fears and the worries of an educated layman. He clearly believed in a satanic conspiracy. Writing at a time when witch hunting was at a peak, he anxiously noted: 'The sin of witchcraft and devilry has prevailed, and cannot be gotten discovered and purged out, Satan having set up his very throne among us.' In April 1662 Lord Brodie was involved with a case at Forres where two women retracted confessions made earlier. When they were tortured and beaten, Brodie was perturbed and was 'in great darkness of soul about the matter.' But, when they, on being condemned to death, continued to deny their guilt, Brodie prayed 'Lord, overcum their obduredness.' Despite his prayers, the women died 'obstinat'.

Some accused witches, it would seem, confessed without use of torture. One such was Isobel Gowdie of Auldearn. Like John Philp, she fantasised about being in league with the Queen of the Fairies. 'I was in Downie Hills, and got meat there from the Queen of the Fairies more than I could eat. The queen is brawly clad in white linen, and in white and brown cloth . . .' In her confession she told, too, that she had met the devil who 'was a meikle, black, roch man.' But he could transform

himself into a deer or a crow and indeed could come to
her in any shape. Although sometimes he wore boots and
sometimes shoes, his feet were forked and cloven. Not only
did she become his servant but she copulated with him. He was
'very cold and I found his nature [semen] within me as cold as
spring-well-water.'

With other witches Isobel Gowdie formed a coven (her
confession provides the first recorded use of the term) who,
as her judges evidently believed, wrought havoc in the area with
their mischief-making and malicious acts. Houses (including the
Earl of Moray's abode) were entered and food and drink stolen,
the barrels being filled up again 'with our own pish'. Elf-arrows
(which she had seen being shaped and trimmed in Elfland) were
employed to destroy beasts and men and women too. A long
list of the covens' 'victims' is provided. In 1660 the coven, she
confessed, attempted to kill the minister of Auldearn, the Rev
Harry Forbes, when he was sick. The Laird of Park and his sons
were also targets. An accomplice, who was also interrogated,
described how the witches of Auldearn made a noxious stew
from dog's and sheep's flesh. After the devil had stirred the
mixture with his own hands, the witches scattered the pieces
in places where the male members of this family were liable
to go. If any of them touched or stood on the devil's meat,
death was inevitable. And indeed it was the witches' boast that
they had thus accomplished the death of the last two lairds
of Park.

The Auldearn witches' confessions probably reflect, on the
one hand, popular myths and old wives' tales about the devil
and, on the other hand, the subject-matter of sermons and
other admonitions on the perils of satanism. How often, one
wonders, had Isobel Gowdie heard her minister, the Rev Harry
Forbes, preach on the subject of witchcraft? Did her confessions
derive from, in T. C. Smout's words, 'the hallucinations of a
mind that had cracked under Calvinist bombardment'? For
Harry Forbes, as with Lord Brodie, Satan was an ever-present
and very real threat. In 1655 the year he became minister at
Auldearn, Harry Forbes told Alexander Brodie of his crusade
against witches. On a previous occasion some witches had
sought his life. But he asserted: 'they could doe him no harm;
made his image of wax but could not hurt him.' Did this story

and others of a like nature help create and shape the witchcraft culture of Auldearn and neighbourhood?

We don't know what happened to Isobel Gowdie, although, with the Rev Harry Forbes as one of the trial commissioners, acquittal would have been unlikely. Almost certainly she would have suffered the same fate as two confessed witches at Elgin. These two, Barbara Innes and Mary Collie, were tried in that same year in November 1662. There were 25 men on the jury and another 11 sat on the bench. As the judges included the Provost and Baillies of Elgin, the Sheriff of Moray and the Bishop of Moray, it is evident that the ruling elite took witchcraft very seriously. With one exception, the jury found the accused women guilty of 'paction with the devil'. They were sentenced to be taken out through the West Port and then strangled and their bodies and bones burned to ashes. The dissenting juryman was Colonel Lachlan Rose of Loch. He was declared to be 'ignorant'.

According to local tradition, another Morayshire laird, was regarded as a warlock. In truth, this 17th-century laird, Sir Robert Gordon of Gordonstoun (which is now a celebrated private school), was a scholar of note whose scientific experiments and other investigations seem to have been misinterpreted by untutored locals. Beholding the lights of Gordonstoun shining forth late into the night, credulous countryfolk firmly believed that Sir Robert was holding court with the devil. When their evening's carousing was done, they said, the devil turned himself into a coal-black charger. The Laird of Gordonstoun then clambered onto this fiercesome mount and galloped off to join in witches' revels in the auld kirkyard of Birnie. With Sir Robert only his reputation was at risk, but too many lower class unfortunates — mostly women, it should be noted — received treatment that, by any standard, was truly abominable.

Folk memory has preserved the name and location of different gallows hills and other places of punishment. Among them are a number of places where, according to tradition, witches were executed or tested as to their guilt by being thrown into a deep pool. Elgin once had its Order (ie. Ordeal) Pot — a pond where witches, it was popularly thought, were put to the ordeal. A similar tradition is attached to a deep pool, the Gaun's Pot, in the River Isla at Keith. Alleged witches, when

Witches' Stone at Forres. (Photograph: the author)

cast into the water, were deemed guilty if they managed to stay on the surface. If they sank, they were reckoned to be innocent! At the east end of Forres, near the police station, a stone clamped with iron can be seen by the roadside. According to local legend, witches were squeezed into barrels through which spikes were driven and then rolled down Cluny Hill. The stone supposedly marks the spot where one such barrel came to a halt. And, also according to local tradition, that was the place where the barrel and its human contents were burned.

Still, not all so-called witches were put to any kind of trial. After all, belief in the supernatural, and many rites, survived centuries of official disapproval and condemnation. In rural and fishing communities especially, old beliefs lingered on — long enough to be noted and collected by assiduous Victorian-age folklorists. In Victorian Buckie, for example, it was customary for water to be taken from the sea on New Year's Day and then sprinkled over the fireplace. This was using seawater as a protective charm. Practices like this have a long history. But in 1674, when Margaret Spence in Banff used seawater in a somewhat similar way, she incurred clerical disfavour. Her offence was that, in time of morning prayer, she had cast water seven times from the sea towards the town and had thrown five stones into the sea. (While the seawater purified, throwing away the stones removed evil elements from the land.) Having been detected, she was clearly aware of the dangers she faced. 'On her soul's salvation,' she swore, 'this had been done just to prevent the fever.' Fortunately for her, Margaret Spence was one of the lucky ones, and she was merely rebuked.

If witches like Isobel Gowdie were seen as social irritants, so too were the gipsies or 'Egyptians' as they were termed. Successive punitive acts condemned them as vagabonds. The most notorious of these rovers was James Macpherson who led, it was alleged, an armed gang which terrorised the population. The outlaw is commemorated by a tune, Macpherson's Rant, and by a ballad or, since there are several versions, ballads. Arrested by Duff of Braco at Keith in 1700, Macpherson and one of his accomplices were brought before the Sheriff of Banff and condemned to be hanged. According to tradition, Macpherson, who was an expert fiddler, played his last tune beneath the gallows tree and, defiant to the last —

He took the fiddle intae baith o his hands
An he brak it ower a stane.
Says no anither hand shall play on thee
When I am deid an gane.

The two gipsies were hanged on a gibbet erected at the cross of Banff in November 1700. A tradition that a pardon being on its way the burgh clock was advanced has no foundation in fact. More prosaically the Banff burgh records reveal that £1 was paid to the executioner for tous (or rope). The ballads, nevertheless, may well reflect contemporary opinion. The swashbuckling Macpherson probably did attract a great deal of sympathy. It was after all a time of famine when many smallholders and day-labourers were forced into beggary. Apart from gipsies, there were hordes of poor folk who, during these 'ill years', turned to vagrancy through no fault of their own. So Macpherson came to be seen as a

Banff's mercat cross, which has been moved around over the years, is topped by a fine 16th century crucifix. (Photograph: the author)

folk-hero and, thanks to the balladeers, became the stuff of legend.

> Sae rantinly, sae wantonly,
> Sae dantinly gaed he.
> He played a tune, an danced it roon,
> Ablow the gallows tree.

CHAPTER 4

The Jacobite Risings and Their Aftermath

'At the Revolution, the palace [Spynie] and precinct were annexed to the crown ... The lessees or tacksmen have carried away, and sold all the iron and wood-work; so that the bare walls only remain of this stately building; and these are now in great ruin, being demolished to obtain the lime mortar for the neighbouring farm-lands.' (Survey of the Province of Moray', 1798).

The Revolution of 1689, which sealed the fate of the bishop's former residence at Spynie, had accomplished the deposition of James VII and II. Once again though opinion in the three counties was divided. While the Presbyterian Brodies and Roses gave thanks for delivery from the rule of the 'Papists', the Gordons remained loyal to the Stewarts. But the head of the clan, who had been elevated to a dukedom by Charles II, stayed neutral when Viscount Dundee took up arms on behalf of James VII. By then the once palatial Huntly Castle had been abandoned and successive 'Cocks of the North' had spent heavily on their house at Fochabers, Bog of Gight or Gordon Castle as it was later termed. The death at Killiecrankie of the charismatic Bonnie Dundee was an immense blow to the Jacobite cause and in the following year (1690) the last of the insurgents were surprised and routed, with the help of the Strathspey Grants, at the Haughs of Cromdale, due east of Grantown.

The overthrow of King James meant that once again the bishops were sent packing. With the Presbyterian Kirk supreme at last, clergymen whose loyalty was suspect were deposed. In a time of general bigotry, the provost and magistrates of Elgin displayed a remarkable degree of tolerance by dividing the parish kirk and permitting the lesser part, the 'Little Kirk', to be utilised as an episcopalian place of worship. The main part from 1690 onward, of course, housed a presbyterian congregation.

In those districts where there were many Episcopalians and Roman Catholics, the ousted clergy received a great deal of sympathy and support. Banffshire was just an area. Whereas in 1677 there were, according to a contemporary estimate, only 50 Catholics in Glasgow and neighbourhood, there were 1000 in Banffshire. In contrast only 8 were listed for Moray. The Banffshire Catholics were strongest in Strathavon and Glenlivet and in the Enzie, which is in the north-west corner of the county roughly between Buckie and the Spey. The still powerful Gordon family protected their co-religionists and browbeat and threatened intruding Presbyterians.

Not surprisingly, the Banffshire lairds and populace did not take kindly to ecclesiastical change. There was a great deal of opposition and a lot of stalling which ensured that some Episcopalian clergymen, despite refusing to swear loyalty to the new monarchs, managed to stay in their parishes. In the parish of Rathven (which includes Buckie), the Rev John Hay had been deposed in 1694 for refusing to pray for William and Mary. Receiving strong support from all classes, John Hay, however, continued to minister to the folk of Buckie and neighbourhood. When the presbytery of Fordyce tried to instal Presbyterian ministers, the heritors and elders prevaricated and put all sorts of obstacles in their way. When eventually in 1700 a Presbyterian clergyman, William Chalmer, was intruded, the parishioners, encouraged by their lairds, rioted. The presbytery complained that their nominee had been abused 'by a rabble which had fallen upon him, offered violence to his person, pulling from him his hat, cloak, and gloves, blacking and scratching his face, stoning him with stones, so as he had not access to the church, but was forced to preach in James Coull's house.'

When Chalmer left after four fruitless years, the presbytery endured more prevarication and intermittent violence and, not surprisingly, couldn't find a clergyman brave enough to face the wrath of the parishioners of Rathven. In 1715, 21 years after the deposition of John Hay, the issue was still not settled. The presbytery had, however, found a candidate for Rathven but one who had to be ordained in the kirk at Boyndie 15 miles away. When the new minister, the Rev Robert Gordon, did appear at Rathven, he was accompanied by the Sheriff-Depute and 'a considerable company, both of gentry and commons in arms'. Nevertheless, they found that the kirk had been locked and the approaches to it barred by a huge mob of men and women who threw stones and cursed and swore. Forcing their way in, the escort was able to hear Mr Gordon preach his first sermon while the howling mob that comprised his congregation stayed outside.

A few months later the troubles at Rathven were subsumed in the much greater disturbances occasioned by the Jacobite rising which started in September 1715. During the '15 the Rev Robert Gordon kept well away from his turbulent parishioners. In 1716 after the rising was over, he returned to the parish of Rathven. But he found the fisher folk and farmers of the Buckie area to be no more amenable than before. True some had been converted from episcopacy, but they went the other way — more than a third of the population of Rathven becoming 'Papists'. Not surprisingly, the strain affected the minister. In May 1719 Robert Gordon intimated to the congregation that for the recovery of his health he was going to the Highlands to try the goat milk cure. The poor state of the kirk 'for four winters past' also affected his health. He died in November 1720. One wonders how many of his parishioners recalled the threats made six years prior — that if the presbytery were to proceed with his ordination, they should 'bring his coffin and winding sheet with them.'

During these years of religious and civil disputes, there were other issues and changes that affected the folk of the north-east. Crop failures posed a major threat as in October 1687 when the clergy of the north-east were ordained to hold a solemn fast on account of 'the sad and deplorable condition of the corns and fruits of the ground be reason of the great deluge of rains which hath fallen out and the constant fogges and mists which have continued since the harvest began.' With harvesting coming later in those days, the crops in many places were still in the fields.

This was a period of climatic deterioration — the so-called 'little ice age'. When in the late 1690s temperatures reached their nadir, the high Cairngorms, according to travellers' accounts, were permanently capped with snow. Very bad weather, even worse than in 1687, caused havoc, with the Highlands and upland areas of the north-east — the Cabrach for instance — being particularly badly affected. Within the period 1695 to 1700, when there was a series of bad harvests, there were three disastrous years — described by Jacobite propagandists as 'the black years of King William'. During these 'ill years', famine, and famine-related illness and disease, made a devastating impact, causing many deaths. In Aberdeenshire, which was one of the worst affected areas, it has been estimated that one person in four died either of starvation or of famine-related disease. Soaring food prices, coming at a time of trade depression, made a terrible situation even worse. Upland farms were abandoned and beggars swarmed into the towns and villages. Although writing a hundred years later, the minister of Duthil in Strathspey gave a vivid account of the horrors of famine: 'The poorer sort of folk frequented the church-yard, to pull a mess of nettles, and frequently struggled about the prey, being the earliest spring greens, which they . . . boiled without meal or salt. So many families perished from want, that, for 6 miles in a well inhabited extent, within the year there was not a smoke remaining. Nursing women were found dead upon the public roads, and babes in the agonies of death sucking at their mother's breasts.'

Although the Laich of Moray and coastal Banffshire may have suffered less damage, the parish of Drainie must have been hit rather badly. In 1699, to provide relief for the poor of the parish, the landowners were assessed (i.e. taxed according to their wealth). While landowners were usually opposed to assessment, in this case it was the alleged wizard, Sir Robert Gordon of Gordonstoun, who took the initiative. Sir Robert, it should be said, owned two-thirds of the parish. Grange in Banffshire also suffered heavily, as the parish registers indicate that, during the famine period, there was a marked decrease in the number of marriages and, subsequently, of baptisms. The session records of Fordyce also provide some clues as to the measures taken by the authorities, or rather the lack of them. They reveal, according to a later incumbent, that no extraordinary measures were taken to aid the destitute, except towards the end. This clergyman, writing in the 1790s, did notice that — 'The thing most remarkable was, that for several years before the famine, adultery and fornication had been extremely frequent, to which the famine put an entire and speedy stop.' In those days, of course, the unco guid of the kirk sessions diligently pursued and punished such moral offenders.

The 1690s saw another disaster, albeit a localised one. This occurred when the barony of Culbin in Moray was buried in sand. For some years sand blown from nearby dunes had been encroaching on this once prosperous estate. Then in or around 1694 a great gale blew unparalleled quantities of sand onto the barony lands, overwhelming fields, farm-buildings and manor-house. While the inhabitants managed to escape, their homes and livelihoods were gone. The records of the Parliament of Scotland reveal that in July 1695 the unfortunate laird of Culbin, Alexander Kinnaird, successfully petitioned that he be absolved from paying cess. As he stated in his petition, 'the best two parts of his estate of Culbin, by an unavoidable fatality, was quite ruined and destroyed, occasioned by great and vast heaps of sand (which had overblown the same), so that there was not a vestige to be seen of his manor-place of Culbin, yards, orchards, and mains thereof, and which within these twenty years were as considerable as many within the county of Moray.' (For 150 years and more neighbouring proprietors and latterly the Forestry Commission have reclaimed by judicious planting much of the former Culbin desert. The pinewoods of the Culbin Forest are now a nature reserve.)

It would be wrong, however, to highlight only the disasters and sadder aspects of 17th century society. In both town and country there was a great deal of vigorous growth and development. Even in periods of particular difficulty some managed to prosper, including the Banffshire laird who secured the arrest of James Macpherson. This was the shrewd and avaricious Alexander Duff of Braco (1652–1705). Braco acquired a lot of property by lending to impecunious landowners who in return pledged their estates as surety. Those who couldn't pay up had to surrender their lands. In his own parish of Grange, for instance, the lands that had formerly belonged to Kinloss Abbey had been feued to a great number of small proprietors. When many of these small landowners ran into problems, it was Alexander Duff who acquired most of the feus. An alleged Braco prophecy that he would make the 'reek o the hale countryside come a oot at ae lum' was nearly fulfilled as, according to the minister of Grange who was writing in 1791, 'four-fifths of the whole are now in the hands of his descendants.'

When his son died leaving no heir, Alexander Duff's property passed to his younger, and equally acquisitive, brother William who was already the laird of Dipple and possessed, too, a town-house in Elgin. This arcaded building, long known as Braco's Banking House, still adorns the High Street of Elgin. This dwelling, like other fine 17th century buildings in Elgin, Banff and elsewhere, indicates that civil and religious strife did not impede civic development and, indeed too, some measure of commercial progress. Alexander Duff of Braco represented Banffshire in the Scottish Parliament from 1689 until his death in 1705. Two years later this parliament met for the last time. As luck had it, the Chancellor who presided over the last session was another Banffshire landowner, that egregious place-man the Earl of Seafield. While for Seafield it may have been 'ane end of an auld sang', the abolition of the Scottish Parliament in 1707 and the union with England were highly unpopular. Thus the Jacobites were also able to harness thwarted nationalism; and, as the protracted troubles at Rathven showed, there was a very strong pro-Episcopalian and Roman Catholic sentiment in the north-east, which the supporters of James Francis Edward Stewart (the Old Pretender) were able to tap.

Although many of the lairds supported the '15 rising, it is likely that many of the lesser folk were reluctant conscripts. Even the leader of the rebels, the Earl of Mar, had to use threats and intimidation to get his tenants at Kildrummy into the field. The Laird of Altyre sent a party of rebels into nearby Forres who forced the Town Clerk to proclaim James VIII as the lawful monarch. When later obliged to explain his actions, he insisted that it was 'ill arguing with a Highlander's dirk at your throat.' Other lairds, like William Duff of Braco, temporised although he strengthened 'for his own security' the old castle of Balvenie which had been one of Alexander's many acquisitions.

Influenced by the pro-Hanoverian Roses of Kilravock, the townsfolk of Nairn stayed loyal and indeed contributed to a loyalist force which on the 13th of November seized Inverness. On the very same day Mar, who was an incompetent commander, was checkmated at Sheriffmuir and thus threw away the best chance for success that the Jacobites were to have. When James himself arrived, landing at Peterhead in December

Braco's Banking House on Elgin High Street. (Photograph: the author)

1715, the momentum had been lost and all chances of success had gone.

When the rising collapsed, the Jacobites of the north-east had to go on the run. Some, like General Alexander Gordon of Auchintoul in Marnoch, were eventually permitted to return. A skilful commander, who had learned the arts of war in the service of the Russian Czar, he was, however, too old to fight when Prince Charles Edward Stewart led another Jacobite rising in 1745. There was little enthusiasm in the north-east for this foolishly-conceived enterprise. The erstwhile Lord Braco, now Earl of Fife, had his eldest son forcibly restrained to keep him out of the rebel camp. The Duke of Gordon (a title dating back to 1684) stayed out, although a brother Lord Lewis Gordon eventually joined as did some of the Banffshire Gordons. The Presbyterian ministers were hostile and helped to counterbalance the 'great threatenings' employed by Lord Lewis Gordon to raise men and, equally important, to obtain the money that was required to pay and supply them.

After initial successes which took him as far south as Derby, the Young Pretender retreated north again, with the Hanoverian army under the Duke of Cumberland in pursuit. As Cumberland's men marched through the north-east counties, the retreating Jacobites kept a watchful eye on their advancing enemy. Charles himself lodged for some days at Elgin in Thunderton House. Some of his officers were billeted in the manse of Speymouth Parish Kirk. Although the minister, together with his congregation, was loyal to King George and even prayed for him at a service when several Jacobites were present, the rebels made no protest and indeed treated him 'very civilly'.

Meantime, the Duke of Cumberland had advanced from Aberdeen via Banff to the eastern banks of the fast-flowing River Spey. As they held the other bank, the Jacobites might have been able to do serious damage to Cumberland's forces when they tried to ford the river. (There was no bridge then.) But Lord John Drummond, the officer in charge, made no attempt to oppose the Hanoverians. He justified his decision on the grounds that the river was low at the time and that, furthermore, his artillery was no match for Cumberland's. The

King's army was therefore able to cross the Spey, the last serious obstacle on the road to Inverness, at a point (which is still known as Cumberland's ford) east of Speymouth kirk. The minister of Speymouth had a politically more congenial guest that night, the Duke of Cumberland.

The Hanoverian army pursued the Jacobites and, despite rebel opposition, entered Nairn. The next day being Cumberland's birthday his troops were feasted. That night the Prince led his half-starved and diminished army towards Nairn on an attempt at a night attack. As with General Hurry's attack on Montrose in 1645 in nearly the same area, complete surprise proved to be a chimera. The march was a confused affair and, with the night well gone, the rebels were too far from the enemy camp to have any hopes of achieving surprise. To be realistic, a night attack offered the only chance of success, although it was but a slender hope and, even if successful, would merely have postponed the defeat that was virtually inevitable. On the next day the 16th of April 1746, at Drummossie Moor near Inverness the clans, after being blasted by Cumberland's artillery, made their last brave but futile charge. The defeat at Culloden shattered the rebel clans. Their defeat destroyed Prince Charles' dream of restoring his father to the British throne. The '15 had started in the north-east when Mar raised James' standard at Braemar and now, as fate had it, the battle which decided the fate of his dynasty had been lost in the north-east.

The disarming of the clans and the construction of Fort George, that formidable fortress that was strategically located between Nairn and Inverness, belong more properly to histories of the Highlands, as do the atrocities and savage retribution inflicted by the victors. The author of the Old Statistical Account for Banff (1797) tells us, though, that 'a poor fellow from the country, whose imprudent curiosity led him to mark by notches on his staff, the number of British ships passing in the bay, was apprehended as a spy, and hanged by the King's troops, without the formality of trial.' Nevertheless, when the folk of Banff heard the news of Cumberland's victory, they lit a celebratory bonfire at the market cross. Those who suffered the most were the ordinary recruits, many of whom were not volunteers but had been pressed

The 18th century Roman Catholic seminary for priests at Scalan in Glenlivet. (Photograph: the author)

into service by clan chiefs or their officers. John Gordon of Glenbuchat, for instance, had forced into service men from the Gordon estates. A veteran campaigner, Glenbuchat had fought as a boy at Killiecrankie and had been 'out' again in the '15. He was described on the field of battle as 'an old man, much crouched on a little grey beast'. Before escaping to the continent he witnessed, from a place of concealment, the firing of his home. (St Bridget's farm near present day Tomintoul was built on the site.) Like a number of other leaders, Glenbuchat went on the run. Disguised as a beggar, this 74 year old rebel, who had a price of £1000 on his head, escaped to Norway before finding his way to France where he died in 1750. Other younger rebels, like Alexander Hay of Rannas, were eventually pardoned and restored to their estates.

Those taken captive were very badly treated and many died in captivity. William Jack from Elgin survived to tell of the fate of his friends who, like him, had been incarcerated on prison-ships. 'There is none in life that went from Elgin with me, but William Innes of Fochabers. James Brander Smith

in Conloch dyed seven months agoe. Alexander Frigg dyed
in Cromarty Road. Jo Kintrea that lived in Longbridge dyed
also . . .'

Among the wounded at Culloden was Father John Tyrie,
a Catholic priest from Strathavon who served as chaplain to
Glenbuchat's regiment. At least, unlike many of the men on
the field with him, Father Tyrie had been an eager volunteer.
The Roman Catholic and Episcopalian clergy, however, had to
pay for their loyalty to the Stewart cause. As they were seen,
with justification in some cases, as agents of Jacobitism, existing
legal restraints were reinforced. Their places of worship were
destroyed as, for example, the barn utilised by the Catholics of
Enzie. The Episcopalian chapels at Banff and at Arradoul near
Buckie suffered a similar fate. In remote Glenlivet a seminary
for training Roman Catholic priests had been established at
Scalan in or around 1714. Perceived as a centre for Jacobite
conspiracy, it had been assailed on several occasions before
the '45. The small turf-built college was attacked and burned
again in 1746, but training was afterwards resumed albeit in an
inadequate hovel. In 1762 a nearby farmhouse was taken over
and enlarged. The seminary, aptly described as 'the heartbeat
of Scottish catholicism,' survived until 1799 when training was
transferred from the Braes of Glenlivet to Aquhorties in
Aberdeenshire. In lower Banffshire St Ninian's chapel (1755)
at Tynet between Buckie and Fochabers is the oldest post-
Reformation Roman Catholic place of worship in Scotland.
Its simple unobtrusive design exemplifies the problems created
for Catholics by the Penal Laws of the 18th century. Since in
the years after Culloden, Catholics had to gang warily, this
humble single storey building resembles a cottage-cum-steading
rather than a church. The Church of Scotland had long shown
concern about the strength of Catholicism in lower and upper
Banffshire and made general appeals for money to finance
their missionary endeavours. Kirk members in the Fife burgh
of Inverkeithing, for instance, contributed in 1729 and again in
1764 to a fund 'for propagating the Protestant Religion in the
Enzie.'

As time passed the legal restraints on Episcopalians and
Catholics were less rigidly applied. The nearby Italianate St
Gregory's at Preshome (1788) shows that the local Catholics had

regained their confidence even before the act of 1793 which removed some of their legal disabilities. By that time, also, the Rev George Donaldson, the then incumbent at Rathven, could make kindly and appreciative references about his Episcopalian and Roman Catholic equivalents. His colleague at Kirkmichael was regrettably rather less charitable, but then, while his Catholic rival had got 'an elegant meeting-house', he had to preach in a kirk that was the reverse of elegant.

More influential than size and numbers warranted the Enzie district gave no fewer than 9 bishops to the revived Scottish Catholic Church. Between Protestant and Catholic mutual tolerance became the rule, although when in 1857 the Catholics built a splendid cathedral-like chapel in Buckie, some Presbyterians described its twin spires as the 'twa horns o the Deil'. In the same century substantial Catholic kirks were erected in other north-east towns — at Dufftown, for example, in 1825, Keith in 1832, and Elgin in 1844. As impressive as any, however, for its history and the charm of its sensitively restored interior is 'the Banffshire Bethlehem' of St Ninian's at Tynet.

There were other social and economic changes that followed the Jacobite risings. The roads and bridges built from 1724 by General Wade and successors will be outlined in the chapter devoted to transport. An English concern, the York Buildings Company, purchased some of the rebel leaders' forfeited estates. In their endeavours to maximise profits, this company made some monumental errors. In 1736, for instance, iron mines were sunk in Upper Banffshire by the River Conglass near Tomintoul. But the problems involved in transporting ore and fuel rendered the enterprise uneconomic. (In the mid-19th century the mine was worked again for a few years when manganese was extracted.) The company also exploited the pine forests of Strathspey, the timber being floated down the Spey to the port of Garmouth. Some local landowners followed suit. One by-effect was the growth of ship-building at Speymouth. The centre of activity for this industry was the village of Kingston, a name bestowed by the pioneer shipbuilders who had come to Speymouth from Kingston-on-Hull in Yorkshire in 1786. When the incomers gave up, locals took over. With the decline in demand for wooden sailing ships and a diminished local supply of timber, ship construction at Speymouth came to an end in the 1880s. Thus Speymouth, where Charles II had landed away back in 1650, saw the end of the last, admittedly tenuous link, with the post-Jacobite era of economic change and development.

CHAPTER 5

Auld Touns and New Villages

'Murray is, indeed, a pleasant country, the soil fruitful, watered with fine rivers, and full of good towns, but especially of gentlemen's seats, more and more remarkable than could, indeed, be expected by a stranger in so remote a part of the country . . . As the country is rich and pleasant, so here are many rich inhabitants, and in the town of Elgin in particular; for the gentlemen, as if this was the Edinburgh . . . for this part of the island, leave their Highland habitations in the winter and live here for the diversion of the place and plenty of provisions; and there is, on this account, a great variety of gentlemen for society . . . This makes Elgin a very agreeable place to live in . . .'

This description was penned by Daniel Defoe who, when union was being mooted around 1700, visited Scotland as an agent for the English government. But Elgin, with its royal castle and cathedral, had been an important administrative centre long before this. Although by the late 16th century these focal buildings were no longer functional, Elgin weathered the social and economic shock of the Reformation. The presence in the 1580s of a goldsmith and a surgeon indicates a measure of consumer demand. Judging by the amount of burgh stent (i.e. national tax) paid, Elgin was more prosperous than Forres, Nairn, Cullen or Banff. Stent, it may be said, was based on the estimated wealth of the various royal burghs. By 1705, Elgin had reached, according to the stent roll, 9th place in the tax roll of the Scottish burghs. Since the local merchants exported grain, malt and salmon, it is clear that the fruitful soil and fine rivers, so admired by Defoe, provided the economic basis for the burgh's success.

The status of Elgin as a trading community was reflected in the number of fine buildings that were erected for secular use. Fortunately, a number of good vernacular town houses have survived 19th and 20th century commercial expansion and spoliation. At the east end of the High Street there are some attractive late 17th century arcaded dwellings which include Braco's Banking House. The pediments of the dormer windows of this dwelling display the initials of the original owners — John Duncan and his spouse Margaret Innes and the date 1694. (As married women then — and for long afterwards — kept their own names, the surname initials are different.) Sometimes only part of a house was retained as, for example, at the Tower Hotel which incorporates the stairtower of a dwelling built by Alexander Leslie, an early 17th century baillie. His initials (AL) and his wife's (IB: she was Jean Bonyman) can be discerned on a heraldic panel on this attractive projecting tower. Another interesting old dwelling, Thunderton House, off Thunderton Place, has also been converted into a hotel. Built on the site of the former 'Great Lodging' of the Scottish kings, this was the town mansion of successive county families and, as has been noted elsewhere, was occupied by Prince Charles Edward Stewart prior to Culloden.

Thunderton House is situated in Thunderton Place, one of the medieval lanes that lead off from the High Street. Where the High Street broadens, markets were once held. This too was where the tolbooth (demolished in 1843) and parish kirk and cemetery were located. The market cross stood in the graveyard until 18th century improvers covered over the graves and removed the cross. Although the present Muckle Cross is a Victorian restoration, it incorporates the lion from the old cross. The medieval parish kirk was demolished and replaced in 1828 by the present imposing, Greek-style St Giles kirk.

If we can believe the comments made by various tourists, late 18th century Elgin was a town in decline. According, for instance, to James Boswell, it was 'a place of little trade, thinly inhabited'. The description of the town given in the Old Statistical Account (1791–2) provides some confirmation. The malt trade had gone and the once thriving glove manufacture was 'much on the decline.' On the other hand, the number of shops had greatly increased, there being no fewer than 44. But, as the clergyman who wrote the account lamented, they sold mainly imported goods. Forres, on the other hand, seemed to be reasonably prosperous and it was then, if the parish clergyman's figures are correct, more populous than its old rival of Elgin. The Forres folk, however, the minister lamented, spent too much on dress. Males by then had abandoned the old-style blue bonnets and switched to wearing hats.

Further to the west at Nairn, the herring and salmon fisheries were prosecuted, with lairds like James Brodie of Brodie and Lord Findlater the principal beneficiaries. In 1773, according to Dr Samuel Johnson, this royal burgh of Nairn was in a state of miserable decay. Yet twenty years later Nairn could boast of its flourishing grammar school. So esteemed was the schoolmaster that: 'Gentlemen from all quarters of the country, and some from England, send their children to be educated here.' There were other hopeful signs — pointers to Nairn's later emergence as a successful watering-place. The burgh, as the parish minister proudly observed in 1793, possessed two very good inns. Although the tourist boom was still in its infancy, the town, he further remarked, was 'remarkably well calculated for sea bathing.' One of the innkeepers even had a bathing-machine for hiring to dookers. Nairn, though, differed from its eastern neighbours in one very important respect. It was a town where two cultures met. For Dr Johnson it was at 'the verge of the Highlands; for here I first saw peat fires, and first heard the Erse language.'

No Gaelic was spoken in Banff, but the Rev Abercromby Gordon, writing in 1797, could point to a 'great increase' in the number of buildings. Indeed many of these buildings still survive and help to make Banff one of the most interesting towns in the north-east. This spurt in construction was indeed fairly recent, since the town had been described a few decades earlier as harbourless and therefore 'not of great importance'. Harbour improvements in the 1770s helped, though, to spur industrial growth. By 1797 there was a shipbuilding yard, a brickworks, a tileworks, a rope and sail factory, a soap and candle works, and a brewery whose strong beer was in great demand even in 'distant parts of the country.' Stocking-frames had been introduced and were used in the manufacture of silk, cotton and worsted stockings. Within the parish of Banff about 560 people were employed in 'the several departments of the work'. Trade and commerce were also flourishing, with 21 trading vessels sailing out of the port. Although the burgh's handsome new kirk still lacked a spire, the town hardly merited the criticism bestowed by an ill-disposed and anonymous rhymster.

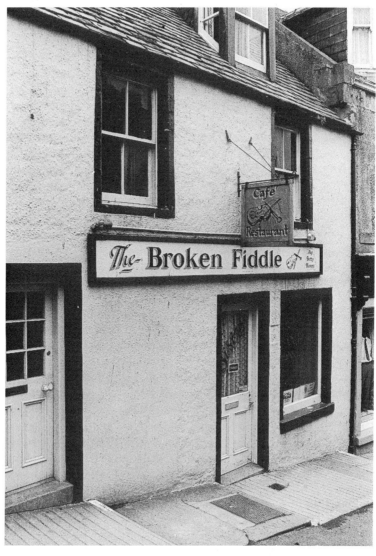

Stepping back into time at Banff. 'The Broken Fiddle' on the historic Strait Path commemorates the execution of Macpherson the outlaw at the nearby Mercat Cross. (Photograph: the author)

'Banff it is a borough's toon
A Kirk withoot a steeple,
A midden o dirt at ilky door,
A very unceevil people.'

In truth, this historic royal burgh attracted either as
permanent or seasonal residents 'many genteel, opulent,
and respectable families.' It was the genteel residents who
would have patronised the dancing assemblies that were held
every fortnight during the winter season and who sent their
daughters to the 'two reputable boarding-schools' that had
been established for the education of young ladies. The
upper ranks of society were very consumer conscious. In
1797 'the art millinery,' for instance, 'affords employment
and profit to many; and every trading vessel from London
brings a fresh assortment of dresses, adjusted to the prevailing
mode.' There were, nevertheless, some disadvantages. With
the end of the Napoleonic Wars in 1815, there were many
retired officers seeking moderately priced accommodation.
While the county town of Banffshire, 'a then charming and
gay resort', appealed to many of these pensioners, there was,
it was claimed, no land available for building in Banff. The
town was hemmed in by the estates of the major landowners,
Lords Fife and Seafield. As these proprietors were at that
time reluctant to make land available for feuing, there was no
suitable space for the erection of 'suburban villas'. These naval
and military annuitants opted instead for the county town of
Moray, with the consequence that, as G. M. Hossack asserted,
'the making of Elgin was the marring of Banff.' It would be
fair to say, however, that, to the extent that Elgin outstripped
Banff, it was due more to the former's nodal position in the
road network and, later in the century, as a railway centre.
Becoming, in comparative terms, an economic backwater had
compensations, inasmuch as Banff managed to retain, with
aid and guidance from the local Preservation Society, many
doucely handsome houses and other buildings — testaments
in stone to the vigour, taste and eye for proportion of the
Banffers of yesteryear.

During the 18th and early 19th centuries, burghs like Banff
had to face competition from new towns and other trading
centres created by ambitious landowners. Not that this was

Garmouth was once a busy seaport. Charles II, who landed at Speymouth in 1650, signed the Covenants here. (Photograph: the author)

anything new, of course, as a number of non-royal burghs had been established in the early modern period. Few of these earlier burghs of barony or regality achieved any great success — certainly not Fordyce (founded by the Bishop of Aberdeen in 1499), nor Deskford (an Ogilvie foundation of 1698) nor Castletoun of Freuchie (created by the Laird of Grant in 1694). Fordyce, though little more than a hamlet, had a celebrated school which enjoyed a remarkable reputation. Fordyce Academy, a Higher Grade school until 1964, was endowed by a native son who became an Indian Nabob. Even earlier in 1451 the Bishop of Moray had created a burgh of barony at Spynie on the loch of the same name. In the Middle Ages Loch Spynie was a sea loch and, although very shallow and under the bishops' control, it served as a maritime outlet for the merchants of Elgin. Since the channel to the sea eventually became blocked, there was no hope of survival for a burgh on the banks of the now land-locked Loch Spynie. The ports of Findhorn (founded by the Abbot of Kinloss in

1532) and Garmouth near the mouth of the Spey (an Innes creation of 1587) were more successful. Although the royal burghs had a monopoly of foreign trade, these small burghs of barony did have some export trade — duly noted by Thomas Tucker, an English exciseman employed by the Protectorate. In 1655 Tucker reported that from 'Garmouth and Findhorne in Murray-land . . . some 60 lasts of salmon in a yeare are sent out, for which salt is brought in from France, and sometimes a small vessell comes in from Holland or Norway.' Both these ports had major handicaps — fluctuating sandbars and the fickleness both of the tides and of the Rivers Spey and Findhorn. Present-day Findhorn, which is a notable yachting centre, is the third village to bear that name. With 12 vessels registered there in 1842, Findhorn remained a significant port until the extension of the railway system deprived it of its trade. Garmouth fared even worse when the Spey forced a new channel, leaving this quaint village high-and-dry. Its annual Maggie Fair survives as a reminder of its former burghal status.

Nearer the mouth of the Spey stands the neat, two-street village of Kingston. Founded as a port in the 1780s, it became, as we have seen, a ship-building centre. Although the original yard closed in 1815, William Geddie, a local shipwright, restarted building. With others following his example, this small community by the mid-19th century possessed no fewer than seven shipyards and housed, in addition to shipmasters and shipowners, sawyers, shipwrights, coppersmiths, blacksmiths, painters, and riggers. Around 350 ships were built there, ranging from fishing boats to Cape-Horners. But by 1888 this once thriving port was described as 'abounding in decaying shipbuilding yards and empty houses and shops, which are falling into ruins.' One of the last shipbuilders, William Anderson, built a ship, the 'Flora Emily', on spec, but then found great difficulty in selling her. When, having sold her for a pittance, he saw the 'Flora Emily' sailing away from Speymouth, he uttered a bitter farewell — 'Awa, and the deil gae wi ye.'

Apart from Kingston, a surprisingly large number of new or semi-new settlements (over 130) were created in the north-east during the second half of the 18th century and the early part of the 19th. Some like Aberchirder were separate, self-contained villages, others like Bishopmill and New Elgin were in effect satellite villages. This was, of course, the 'age of improvement', when enterprising proprietors and their agents were instigating agricultural changes and were embarking upon new business ventures. As new villages were seen as one way of attracting wealth-producing settlers, landowners were obliged to present an attractive package. When, for instance, Alexander Gordon of Auchintoul wished to create the village which became Aberchirder, he advertised in the 'Aberdeen Journal' in March 1764 that he was ready to feu out part of his estate — 'to form a village near the house of Auchintoul, on the high road from Banff to Huntly, where there is great convenience of stone for building. The place will be plentifully supplied with water and the feuars can be accommodated with firing from the moss of Auchintoul.'

Aberchirder, as with a number of other similar villages, was laid out on a virgin site, with one main street centred on a central square. As Foggieloan, as it is locally called, expanded, subsidiary streets were built in a geometrically regular pattern. The square provided the space that was essential for markets, since Foggie, like other comparable settlements, was designed to serve, and exploit the resources of, its rural hinterland. The agricultural basis for the settlement was made clear when the proprietor stated that land for tilling or for pasture would be available on request. It was equally clear, however, that by inviting 'tradesmen, manufacturers, and others' to apply for feus, he was also seeking to draw other productive settlers to his estate. There could have been no flood of applicants, however, as later advertisements show a substantial cut in the feu duty to be paid. In the 19th century, though, Aberchirder did show some growth. Hand-loom weaving and related forms of industry and also its position as a local market centre gave Foggieloan a temporary boost and brought the population to its 1881 peak of 1312. Presumably hopeful of the future, the inhabitants sought burghal status, which was achieved in 1889 when Aberchirder became a Police Burgh. The late 19th century agricultural slump, however, contributed to Foggieloan's subsequent population decline.

Archiestown on Speyside, founded in 1760, was another of the new villages where the proprietor, Sir Archibald Grant of

Monymusk, tried to develop linen manufacture by recruiting three linen weavers from Huntly and a skilled bleacher from Cullen. Despite giving loans to buy equipment and consulting experts in the field, he couldn't achieve manufacturing success at Archiestown. A catastrophic fire in 1783 didn't help matters either. Even at its peak in 1881 the population of this picturesque village reached no more than 374. On the other side of the Spey, planned road and bridge improvements gave Aberlour, which was created in 1812 by Charles Grant of Wester Elchies, more chance of success. It is now the home of a flourishing and very successful bakery, Walkers of Aberlour. The expansion of whisky distilling was a significant factor in the development of Speyside settlements like Aberlour and Rothes and also of nearby Dufftown. Although 'beautiful and picturesque', Rothes, established in 1766 on rather unpretentious lines by the Earl of Findlater, made little progress until it became, as did the Earl of Fife's Dufftown (1817), one of the major centres for the production of whisky. Further up the Spey, Grantown, which it is perhaps superfluous to add, was a Grant foundation, replaced the unsuccessful Castleton of Freuchie. Intended as a manufacturing centre, Grantown-on-Spey, which dates back to 1763, became instead a very successful inland holiday resort.

Tomintoul, laid out in 1777, was also initially a failure despite its strategic location on the military road which went from Strathdon and Deeside, via the Lecht, to Fort George. In 1794 the new settlement contained just thirty-seven families 'with not a single manufacture to employ them', but who 'all of them sell whisky and all of them drink it.' When Queen Victoria arrived in 1860, she described Tomintoul as 'the most tumbledown, poor-looking place I ever saw — a long street with three inns and miserable, dirty-looking houses and people, and a sad look of wretchedness about it.' But Tomintoul later that century become more accessible and also much neater and cleaner. During the holiday season, this village, which is one of the highest in the Highlands, now attracts quite a number of visitors. Tomintoul was established by the 4th Duke of Gordon, and so too was Portgordon which was started in 1795 with the construction of a harbour. In its heyday this was a busy little port, with grain from the Laich of Moray and lowland

The planned village of Tomintoul was laid out in 1777. In the right foreground there is a vintage tractor; on the left is the author's vintage bike. (Photograph: the author)

Banffshire being exported. It became, too, a successful fishing port until the 20th century when fishing became concentrated at the neighbouring seaports of Buckie and Lossiemouth, which enjoyed the benefit of much larger harbours.

A few miles south-west of Portgordon is another of the 4th Duke's creations — namely, the John Baxter designed village of Fochabers which replaced the former burgh of the same name. Old Fochabers, a late 16th century foundation, was located on the King's highway, close by an important crossing point on the River Spey where in 1720 there were 'fine passage boats'. The town in 1720 had some 600 inhabitants and possessed 'a Grammar School, several good lodgins & inns.' Thirty years later it had gained a court-house and was still flourishing. But old Fochabers was too close to his palatial Gordon Castle residence for his lordship's comfort. Accordingly, the Duke of Gordon decided to remove the inhabitants and demolish the village. When in 1776 the Duke's minions began to buy up the old feus, the inhabitants of the old burgh were reluctant to move. James Ross, principal factor, had anticipated problems —

'I wish the removal of the old Toun was as easily Accomplished as your Grace seems to imagine'. To meet his employer's requirements, Ross declared that 'Every method must be taken to force their removal'. It was not till 1802 that the last of the old feus was finally surrendered. Thirty years later Lord Cockburn, that caustic opponent of needless change, thought new Fochabers too 'regular'. He condemned too the policies of the last two dukes who treated it not as 'a village for villagers', but who instead had used it 'as a kennel' for estate employees and for 'the retired lacqueys and ladies'-maids of the castle and for the natural [i.e. illegitimate] children and pensioned mistresses of the noble family . . .' Although bisected by the present-day highway from Aberdeen to Elgin and Inverness, new Fochabers is a handsome, indeed elegant, village. On the other side of the River Spey from Fochabers, there is a renowned food processing factory — Baxters of Speyside. This firm, which is run by the descendants of a former gardener of the Duke of Richmond and Gordon, has prospered despite having once engaged — on a temporary basis — this writer. As for the once enormous Gordon Castle, it is now greatly diminished in size. It is not open to the public.

The historic, royal burgh of Cullen shared the same fate as old Fochabers and was removed between 1820 and 1830. This burgh was also too close to the 'big hoose', the Earl of Seafield's in this instance. Although in decay because of the decline of the once prosperous linen industry and regarded as an unsightly 'swarm of worthless old houses', old Cullen, like Fochabers, was perhaps too precipitately destroyed. Dr William Cramond was aware, even sixty years later, of lingering resentment over the destruction of this 'worthy old burgh'. The following observations may give some indication of Cramond's own sentiments. 'To demolish and remove, within the space of ten years, a town that had existed for, probably, ten centuries, and had risen to the rank of a Royal Burgh, is an undertaking that at the present day [1882] would be deemed incredible in Scotland; yet such was done to the old town of Cullen, and done, so adroitly, that except a few ill-concealed murmurings, the echoes of which have not yet quite died away . . . no voice was raised to oppose.' But the amenity of Cullen House and the perceived interests of the Seafield

The Earls of Seafield considered that the old royal burgh of Cullen stood too close to the big hoose — seen here from the kirkyard. (Photograph: the author)

family were paramount, and everything was removed except for the parish kirk. When in 1872 a new cross was erected in the town square, parts of the historic market cross, which had been constructed in 1675 by master mason Daniel Ross, were incorporated in it. New Cullen was given straight, albeit rather steep, streets and is admittedly well-ordered and neat. Whether this justified the demolition of old Cullen is another matter. There is no reason why at Cullen, and Fochabers too, the new could not have co-existed with the old. This was what happened at a number of other places, including even Cullen itself. At Cullen the old fishermen's quarter blends very nicely with new Cullen. Fortunately, however, the Seaton of Cullen, with its charming, haphazardly-arranged old dwellings, was far enough away from Cullen House to ensure its survival. While a new harbour opened in 1819 brought prosperity to the fisherfolk of Cullen, 20th century decline brought a major reduction in the number of both boats and fishermen. Today the harbour serves mainly recreational purposes.

In the seatown of Cullen many of the fishers' dwellings have been built gable-end to the sea. Telford's harbour was started in 1817. When the railway and viaducts were built in 1882–84, the line was kept well away from the Earl of Seafield's Cullen House. (Photograph: the author)

New Keith is an example of a new settlement that was added to, and co-existed with, an existing, rather straggling village. This pioneering establishment was a Seafield creation, being founded in 1750 by the Earl of Findlater 'for the good of the country' and presumably, too, for his own financial gain. The rapid success of the new village influenced other landowners to follow Lord Findlater's example. The still surviving Auld Brig, which crossed the River Isla, made Keith a strategic point on the main road from Aberdeen to Inverness. The area had its attractions, at least in the early 18th century, when, according to Sir Robert Gordon of Straloch, 'very many gentlemen of lower rank and some barons have houses here.' While by 1791 the old village, the Kirktoun of Keith, was 'greatly on the decline', new Keith, with over 1,000 inhabitants, was adjudged to be 'a large, regular, and tolerably thriving village.' The very spacious market-place — now Reidhaven Square — was a feature of new Keith. It was necessarily large as, at the time of the September Summereve fair, it was required to

Burghead harbour is still well used. (Photograph: the author)

accommodate masses of cattle and horses. Much less successful was the rival, spaciously laid-out village on the north side of the Isla, known as Fife-Keith. This planned settlement, which was founded in 1817 by the 4th Earl of Fife, was described in 1840 as 'a complete failure'. Greater Keith, however, developed into a prosperous market town and absorbed Fife-Keith when it became a police burgh in 1889. For the townsfolk and the farming community over a wide area, the highlight of the year is the Keith Show, which is one of the largest and most prestigious of the agricultural shows of the north.

Another of Lord Fife's creations, the nearby Newtoun of Newmill was little more successful. The same was true of his Urquhart whose lands the Earl had purchased in 1777 from the Duke of Gordon. Nor did Duffus in Moray (or New Duffus as it was originally known) achieve great eminence, despite its 'neat, regular and cleanly' appearance. With only 32 houses in 1842, the same was true of Dallas. A Gordon-Cumming foundation, this was one of the villages designed, in part at least, to house families who had been cleared from their homes to make way for land reorganisation. This Morayshire village has lagged behind its oft-televised namesake in the state of

Texas. Sir William Gordon-Cumming saw the fishing industry as another potential money-spinner and, accordingly, in 1808 founded, and named after himself, the fishing station of Port Cumming or Cummingstown. While the population in 1831 had reached 197, the bulk of the inhabitants of this 'straggling and dirty village' were quarriers or farm labourers. Although some fisherfolk were enticed to Port Cumming, the absence of a harbour was a handicap, the more especially as the more successful adjacent communities of Burghead and Hopeman were each given this essential facility.

Although William Young's Hopeman, site advertised in 1806, attracted craftsmen and seafarers in almost equal numbers, the 'decay' of its harbour was an impediment during the early stages of development. In 1835 it was described as an 'extremely dirty' but 'regularly built' village. A new proprietor, Admiral Duff of Drummuir, then built a new harbour and thus secured the future of the village. Today, although Hopeman still houses quite a few fishing crews, as with the other smaller ports of the area, their boats are based elsewhere. While the old village of Burghead had possessed an excellent natural harbour, its improvement, with a local consortium raising some of the cash and the government paying the balance, was a major factor in the success of the new model village. The prospectus for the new settlement drew attention not just to its merits as a seafaring centre but also to its suitability for 'such as may incline to build for pleasure, or the convenience of Sea-bathing.' Sadly, as with Fochabers and Cullen, there were losses as well as gains. When in the early 1800s new Burghead was laid out in the then almost mandatory grid-iron plan, half of the ancient Pictish fort was destroyed and much of the rest greatly damaged. The failure of the local elite to protect this site is all the more regrettable, since they must have known that this was a site of great historical interest. As well as developing into a significant fishing and commercial port, Burghead was by 1835 well on its way to becoming a sea bathing resort. Many 'respectable families from Elgin and Forres' arrived each summer — attracted by its 'advantages as a watering-place'. These advantages included a suite of salt-water baths, comfortable lodgings and pleasant sea walks. Business-like summer visitors appreciated, too, the good communications. Sailing ships and steam ships from London, Leith and other ports called at Burghead, and the village enjoyed the benefit, too, of 'a daily post and carriers to and from Elgin'. Communications were further improved when a branch railway line was opened in 1862.

Hopeman, Burghead and other coastal villages were erected or remodelled to try to cash in on the area's very considerable maritime resources. There were already on the coast a number of tiny 'fishtouns', like the Laird of Kinnedar's Stotfield and Causea (i.e. Covesea), where a sheltered hythe or haven allowed fishermen to draw their boats on to the shore. Government encouragement in the form of bounties, and the 19th century herring boom encouraged landowners to build new fishing villages or to extend and refashion existing settlements. In the case of Lossiemouth, the Town Council of Elgin were the instigators, feuing land from the Laird of Brodie in 1698 and beginning construction of a quay at the mouth of the River Lossie five years later. To raise money for their harbour of Lossie, Elgin Town Council despatched John Sinclair, a merchant, to go through the kingdom to collect money from parishes and private persons. Sinclair's reward on returning from this 'very toilsom and fatiguing' journey was to find himself accused of falsifying his accounts and overcharging on expenses.

Lossie's development, as G. A. Dixon has shown, has been misunderstood. Initial development was very slow with little progress until a systematically set out extension, instigated by Provost George Brown of Elgin, was tacked on to the tiny village of Seaton. The name Lossiemouth, used for the first time, was bestowed on the new village. Then, during the 19th century, Lossiemouth saw further expansion when the new Stotfield harbour and the spaciously planned settlement of Branderburgh were built on its northern flank. The 19th century herring boom ensured that this planned settlement, initiated by Colonel Brander of Pitgaveny, paid off. The separate units of Lossiemouth, Branderburgh and Stotfield were united in 1890 when the police burgh of Lossiemouth and Branderburgh was created. Lossiemouth became one of the major fishing towns of the north-east and, within our three counties, is second only to Buckie as a fishing centre.

Away back in the 1790s the Rev George Donaldson speired
for information about the origins of the fisher touns of Buckie
and district. His conversations with elderly residents led him to
conclude that Portnockie went back more than one hundred
years, the first house being built in 1677 by a fisher family
from Cullen. Findochty, on the other hand, was settled in
1716 by fishers who had migrated from Broadsea, Portessie,
Buckie's eastern extremity, was apparently founded in 1727 by
fishermen who had been brought from Findhorn by the Laird
of Rannas. (It should be said, however, that local records refer
to a boat-hythe at Rottinslough in 1594. This name survives in
part, as Portessie is still locally known as the Sloch.) According
to 'a man aged 90, still alive, and a native of this parish,
who helped to man the first boat', the laird built 5 houses
to accommodate the Findhorn fisher families. Although he
couldn't be so precise about the two fishing stations of Easter
Buckie and Nether Buckie (or Buckpool), the former was in
existence by 1723 and the latter by circa 1650. New Buckie,
planned by Cosmo Gordon of Cluny in the 1780s, had the
advantage of adjoining the Seatown where, as prospective
feuars were informed, 'there is now a number of fishing
boats and skilful fishers'. These various settlements prospered
during the fishing boom of Victorian days. Buckie was also
extended in an eastward direction when the shore-hugging
fishing settlements of Gordonsburgh, Ianstown, and Portessie
were absorbed, the first two in 1901 and the last in 1903.
Whereas in 1841 Buckie's population had been 2165, in 1911
there were 8897 inhabitants in the extended burgh.

As elsewhere development depended on the provision of
safe harbour accommodation. At Findochty, Portknockie
and Cullen, the Earl of Seafield's 19th century planned
new 'towns' complemented extensive harbour improvements.
Buckie's Victorian expansion was made possible by the
construction in 1857 of Buckpool harbour (now filled in and
landscaped). It was superseded in 1880 by the commodious
Cluny harbour. Built by John Gordon of Cluny, this harbour
is accessible at all stages of the tide. Another major boon
was the building in the 1880s of the coast railway line.
This ensured that fish landed at the port would be swiftly
transported to southern markets.

In contrast to Buckie's stir and bustle, Crovie, at the eastern extremity of the county, and Sandend, between Cullen and Portsoy, are old-style fishing villages. Sandend (or Sanine in local parlance), with its narrow lanes and cottage-sized houses built gable-end to the sea, is a visual delight. So too is Crovie, which circumscribed by high cliffs, has a single row of cottages precariously perched on a narrow, sea-threatened strip of land. Of the other Banff district ports, Portsoy was created a burgh of barony in 1550. By the early 18th it had a safe harbour and at the end of the century what was rare for an area with no coal a successful saltworks. Its attractive 18th and 19th century warehouses and grainstores point to its former importance as a trading port. As fishing and fishing-related industries grew in importance, Portsoy, like its eastern neighbour Whitehills, prospered until the herring market collapsed after the first World War. Whitehills is unusual among the smaller ports of the north-east inasmuch as its harbour is still regularly used by the fishing boats of the port. In the 1920s the villagers of Whitehills were pioneers in marketing their white fish. Utilising motor vans they were able to reach places and customers that other fish salesmen couldn't reach.

As for Banff itself, it was once a significant fishing port but declined when its harbour silted. Macduff on the other side of the estuary of the River Deveron replaced Banff as the major fishing centre of eastern Banffshire. As a fishing settlement the 'sea toune' of Doune, as Macduff was formerly called, extends far back into the past. Although it had been created a burgh of barony in 1528, this attempt to develop the area's potential failed. James Duff, Lord Macduff and later Earl of Fife, was more successful. It was Lord Fife who changed the name to Macduff. The fact that he himself had helped to build the first harbour was the Earl's explanation for his choice of name for the remodelled village. Writing to his factor in 1781, he observed — 'I think if any change [of name] is made it ought to be Macduff, for when I held that title, I worked more in the harbour with my own hands than ever you did in your whole life.' Securing its re-erection as a burgh of barony in 1783, Lord Fife appointed his factor, William Rose, as Provost, adding 'and you can settle anybody Bailie you please.' The Earl had a burgh cross built with an inscription which erroneously stated that it was a royal burgh. Nevertheless, unlike so many other planned settlements of the time, this new burgh prospered. Whereas there had only been a handful of fishermen's houses in 1732, sixty years later there were 'several well laid out streets and 1000 souls in the town.' Lord Fife's burgh so outstripped Banff as a maritime centre that in 1884 the Customs House was transferred across the Deveron to Macduff. Fishing, boat-building and tourism have ensured that Macduff has, generally speaking, lived up to the hopes of its founder that it may 'flourish, increase in number and opulence, while its inhabitants gain the blessings of life by industry, diligence, and temperance.'

Despite the present state of uncertainty in the fishing industry, my guess is that many of the inhabitants of the most easterly of Banffshire's fishing communities would also claim to have secured the same 'blessings of life'. This is Gardenstown which was founded in 1720 by, and named after, Alexander Garden of Troup. Popularly known as Gamrie (from the parish and bay of the same name), the harbour of this precipitously sited village is used only by small boats. As is the case with practically all similarly sized villages, the larger white fish and prawn catching vessels fish out of Fraserburgh or Peterhead and also make frequent sorties to more distant fishing grounds. The fishing community of Gardenstown — a Plymouth Brethren stronghold — is noted for its strict adherence to traditional religious tenets. Although Sabbath observance is now by no means universal, there are still fishermen in Gamrie, and elsewhere in the north-east, who refuse to sail or fish on Sundays. As all their forebears were once wont to do, 'Christian' fishermen do not leave port until the Sabbath is over. The farmer-cum-journalist, John R. Allan, wrote in that peerless classic 'North-East Lowlands of Scotland' (1952) that a percipient observer said to him — 'When you are accustomed to have nothing but the thickness of a plank between you and a watery grave, you do want to feel that the Almighty's hand is strong to save.' The inimitable John R. Allan, of course, had to add, 'Or, considering the age of some drifters — both hands.'

CHAPTER 6

Town and Country: Farmers and Lairds

'It's nae guid, jist fed up o'it. It's no ill to mak a pound, it's keeping it that's the trouble.'

Speaking these words of disillusionment in a 1991 BBC Scotland programme, a north-east farmer summed up the reasons why he was selling his farm. For him the cold winds, heavy rain, and high rates of interest of the late 1980s were an unlucky combination. In consequence, quite a number of long-established, but over-borrowed, farmers have been forced to sell out to purchasers, mostly affluent incomers from the south.

Depressing though this kind of situation must be, the troubles of the present day are scant in comparison to the disasters and woes that previous generations had to endure. Bank loans may be onerous, but they are preferable to the blackmail once levied by Highland cattle-thieves. Highland caterans taking the 'Thieves' Road' from Glencoe and Lochaber often raided the more fertile north-eastern counties. In this respect a letter of apology from Lochiel, the chief of the Camerons, is singularly revealing. In it Lochiel, writing in October 1645, apologised to his 'respected and loving cousin', the Laird of Grant. His Lochaber clansmen had, by a 'misfortunate accident', raided Grant-owned territory. The Cameron reivers, Lochiel apologetically explained, had thought they were in 'Murray lands where all men take their prey'. Lochiel couldn't have been plainer: the farms of the Laigh o Moray and other lowland districts were legitimate targets. And this state of affairs persisted for another 100 years, right down to the '45. Occasionally, though, the caterans came off second best, as happened in the afore-mentioned 1645 raid. The Grants of Strathspey mustered and conducted a successful pursuit. Not only did they kill eight and wound twelve of the Camerons, but they also retrieved their stolen kye.

As we have seen, too, there were times when poor harvests could be quite literally catastrophic. While famine on the scale

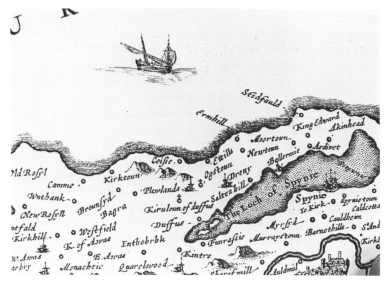

Place-names in use around 1600 as shown on Blaeu's Atlas. Spynie Loch was subsequently reduced in size by land reclamation schemes.

of the 'Ill Years' of the 1690s was not repeated, there were, nevertheless, other years, most notably in the early 1740s and in 1782, when bad harvests caused great suffering. The disasters of the 'dear year' of 1743 and of the 'frosty hairst' of 1782 were long remembered. Even members of the gentry ran into difficulties as when in October 1782 Jean Grant, Lord Fife's mother, had to write to her son imploring assistance in order to feed her household servants. On the other hand, there were quite a few good years when grain from the Laich o Moray and other fertile areas was shipped south to Leith and other Scottish ports and sometimes also exported. Nor indeed was rural society static. There were lairds and other cultivators in the 17th century who were employing practices and techniques that in a later age would have earned commendation. But the later 18th century 'improvers' were inclined to cry doon the agricultural and other achievements of their predecessors. The propagandists of the age of enlightenment convinced not only their contemporaries but following generations also that pre-1707 Scotland was a place of absolute backwardness and darkness. Yet change was underway long before the union. Trees were planted, land was enclosed, and productivity increased by the use of lime and crop rotation. Attempts at land reclamation were also made — on the haughlands and salt marshes at the mouth of the Deveron at Banff, for instance.

Nevertheless, the rate of agricultural change had been slow. Generally, in the early 18th century, fields were open and unenclosed and the large-sized individually-owned or rented farming unit that we know today scarcely existed. Instead there were many multiple-tenancy farms, or ferm-touns, where several farmers shared the land and worked in close cooperation. Although, at least from the 17th century onward, the number of individual holdings had been on the increase, the switch to the single farm, with its enclosed fields, was accelerated during the late 18th and early 19th centuries. While in some academic circles it is no longer fashionable to speak of an 'agricultural revolution', this was certainly a time of far-reaching change.

On the old type of settlement, a four-fold yield was considered satisfactory. The finest crops came from the infield, which was the best land. The infield received most of the available manure and was thus generally kept under constant tillage. We call to witness Alexander Garden of Troup who wrote in 1683 that — 'The husbandman [i.e. farmer] keeps some of his ground constantly under corne and bere [a kind of barley] dunging it every third year.' Of the poorer land, the outfield, as it was termed, only a small part was cultivated in any one year. The rest of the outfield provided rather inadequate grazing for the livestock. Common lands — undrained meadows and uncultivated muirs — were also used for grazing. Upland moorland was separated from the cultivated area by a hill dyke, and this was often the only form of enclosure to be seen. Although frequently classified as waste, much of this common land was potentially fertile.

Because of the system of land tenure, only the lairds could initiate change on any considerable scale. The more far-seeing proprietors realised that reform was necessary. Scrapping the communal forms of tenancy, these 'improving' lairds carved out new enlarged holdings. These were let to the more ambitious tenant-farmers who, if granted long leases, had the incentive to fence-off or otherwise enclose their holdings. Gradually, the semi-communal ferm-touns, with their hamlet-like clusters of dwellings, were swept away. Confusingly, though, the name ferm-toun continued in use, although the new homesteads were built and operated in a very different style.

The most influential of the early improvers was Lord Deskford (1716–70), later the 6th Earl of Findlater. (He was also 3rd Earl of Seafield, a title conferred on that pliable placeman, the 4th Earl of Findlater, for his services to the Crown around the time of the Treaty of Union.) The Seafield estate lands west of Banff were described by a knowledgeable observer as being cultivated like a garden. Wisely realising that, if his estate lands were to be effectively managed, a good factor was essential, Lord Deskford selected an able young man, John Wilson, and despatched him on an agricultural tour of Britain to study, and report on, examples of good practice. Setting an example to his tenants by introducing turnips as a field crop, the Earl raised no objection when he was informed that the locals were stealing his neeps. He retorted — 'That precisely answers my purpose. Having learned their value in this way they will not fail to sow them for themselves.' Amalgamating farms that had previously been occupied by three or four tenants, the Earl granted long leases to carefully selected tenants, on condition that they applied new methods of crop rotation and enclosed their fields with dykes or hedges. Lord Deskford also planted many trees, as did many other proprietors including the 4th Earl of Fife and the 9th Earl of Moray. The latter was aptly called the 'Tree Planter', since by the time of his death in 1810 he had been responsible for planting over 12 million trees on his ancestral estate at Darnaway. While Scots fir predominated, large numbers of oaks and other broad leafed trees were also planted. Later Earls of Moray carried on with this policy of afforestation, for financial reward and to enhance the landscape. In 1841 no fewer than 41 miles of pleasure-walks were constructed in Darnaway forest which, as a contemporary observed, 'for variety, extent, and grandeur of scenery, have few parallels even in this picturesque region.' (By a happy coincidence I can look from my study window on wooded areas that were also planted by past members of the Moray family on their former Donibristle estate in Fife.)

Visitors arrive at Darnaway Castle, seat of the Earls of Moray.
(Photograph: the author)

Obviously, too, improvement for some meant loss for others,
since consolidation of the former multiple-tenancy farms led
to evictions — a gradual form of clearance that attracted little
or none of the opprobrium of the more spectacular Highland
Clearances. The Rev T. McLauchlan, who was a fierce critic of
the west coast evictions, took a kinder view of the clearances in
the straths of Nairn, Findhorn and Spey. In those areas, he
remarked, 'judicious and considerate landlords' had improved
the condition of the remaining population by providing them
with suitable holdings. Some of the evicted tenants found
accommodation, and sometimes too employment, in the new,
planned villages which proprietors like Lord Deskford created
as part of their general strategy for improvement.

Even by the 1790s, as we learn from Sir John Sinclair's
'Statistical Account', large-scale change was the exception rather
than the rule. The old ways, as the clergymen who wrote the
parish reports made only too clear, survived longer in the
upland parishes. At Kirkmichael in Highland Banffshire, the
inhabitants followed 'the practice of their ancestors' except that

they grew considerable quantities of turnips and potatoes. Even as late as the 1830s, the folk of Ardclach in Nairnshire persisted with the traditional infield and outfield system of cultivation. The outfield was cropped in classic fashion, with 'three or four, and sometimes more, grain crops, in close succession, and was then abandoned, to remain for seven years or upwards in a state of nature, overgrown with weeds, and totally unproductive. It was then "tathed" [manured] by folding cattle or sheep upon it, broken up, and cropped as before.'

Ardclach, not surprisingly, had been one of the parishes which suffered from scarcity following the disastrous harvest of 1782. Better local organisation and government help meant that there were comparatively few deaths compared to earlier famines. Improved roads and means of carriage ensured that grain from lowland parishes, like Drainie and Rathven where the crops had done better, was transported to places in need. Even so, as at Ardclach, while there were no deaths 'from want' in the dearth of 1782–3, there were evidently even in normal times many desperately needy people. Although in 1791 there were only 35 paupers on the poor-roll, 'many more might be added.' Poor relief in this parish came from one source only — kirk collections. But the money that was raised by purely voluntary means, as the minister admitted, furnished 'but a scanty allowance.' As in so many other northern parishes, the poor could survive only through begging. One way out was enlistment, generally into local regiments like the Gordon Highlanders but a few 'tall men' from lowland Rathven volunteered, rather more exotically, to enter the service of the King of Prussia. Emigration to North America was another partial solution. Some of the mobile poor headed for towns and villages that were rather nearer hand, but which offered some hope of employment. A readily available source of fuel, as at Nairn where there was a good supply of peat close to the town, attracted needy migrants. Unfortunately, the supply of peat was finite and the exhaustion of this formerly 'excellent peat-moss' helped to 'increase the number of mendicants who [in 1793] infest the place'. Another good peat-moss and also the riches and 'abundance of a very populous and plentiful country' lured 'a colony' of indigent, Gaelic-speaking Highlanders to settle in the parish of Keith. Displaced country-folk made for new villages like Fife-Keith and Newmill where, in addition to a supply of peat, they could rent 'a small croft of land'. Where manufactures had been introduced, as at Keith and Archiestown, there were opportunities for people with specialised skills. The first settlers at Archiestown included weavers from Cullen, Fochabers, Huntly, and Portsoy. Since the proprietor was trying to develop a linen manufactory, John Ogg, a lintdresser, who migrated from Keith, would have been a key worker.

Old burghs, too, like Banff and Cullen benefited from the 18th century boom in linen manufacture. Once again Lord Deskford pioneered by bringing experienced weavers and other experts to the Seafield estates. These experts included an Irish Quaker, John Christie, who in 1752 drew up a plan for a bleachfield. A sizeable area, not to mention considerable capital expenditure too, was required for the buildings and canals needed for the bleaching area and also for the drying field. Although by 1791 the Scottish linen industry was on the downturn, the gains wrought not just in the burgh of Cullen but also in the rural hinterland had been very considerable. 'All the young people were engaged in the business; and even the old found employment in various ways by the manufactures: and thus a spirit of industry was diffused over the place and neighbourhood in a very short time, which soon appeared in their comfortable mode of living, and their dress.' Reminders of this once important, but now long gone, local industry are few. Signposts pointing to the Lintmill of Cullen provide one of the few obvious clues. Water-powered lintmills for scutching or beating flax were one of the innovations in the 18th century linen industry.

At Cullen, as elsewhere in the north-east, textile manufacture was a cottage industry, with very many children and women of all ages contributing in a number of ways. Spinning woollen and, more especially, linen yarn, was an extremely common activity until the development of factory spinning. In the Forres area merchants bought the yarn and sent it south to be sold in Glasgow. The minister of the parish, writing in 1795, testified that the earnings of the considerable number of women employed had been 'of great advantage to themselves, and beneficial to the public.' It was however, as he recognised, a trade that was on the decline 'owing to the increase of machines for spinning cotton in the south country, and the great quantities of yarn from Ireland imported into Glasgow, by which the price of yarn in this country has been greatly reduced.' Significantly, it was cotton that was being spun on the new machines. Linen went into decline, as southern-made cotton fabrics gained in popularity. Nevertheless, the transformation wrought by these government-aided developments had been immense. The rise of the linen industry, including ancillary activities like textile-finishing, brought major benefits to the north-east. Since good bleaching was essential for quality production, other bleachfields were constructed at Banff, Deskford, Forres, and Keith as well as at Cullen. The ports benefited too, since most of the flax was imported.

Many of the part-time workers employed in the textile industry would have been drawn from cottar families. As sub-tenants of the better-off husbandmen, the cottars or cottagers were the people in the lower strata of rural society. Except inasmuch as they all occupied a humble cottage, cottars are difficult to describe and characterise. Many, maybe most, cottars gave their labour to a tenant-farmer in return for a croft or small piece of land and some grazing rights. Some cottars, too, were engaged in other once essential rural crafts, working, often on a part-time basis, as carters, weavers, tailors, masons, shoemakers, carpenters, coopers, wheelwrights, etc. Where demand for specific services was strong, some cottars were able to work as full-time tradesmen. In the north-east a great deal of waste land was reclaimed and cultivated by cottar folk or crofters, as they often came to be called. Later, as conditions changed, croft holdings became uneconomic and very many of them were eventually either cleared or abandoned. While the holdings were absorbed into larger farming units, the cottages were often just left to decay.

Not surprisingly, it was the landowning class that benefited most from the various agrarian and industrial innovations. The increased productivity of the land helped consolidate the already enormous power and authority of the landowners like the Findlaters, Fifes and Morays. Their social and political dominance rested not just on social status but on economic power. In 1770, for instance, over half of the valued rent of

The heart of Cawdor Castle is the 14th century central tower. The castle has been considerably enlarged as a result of additions and extensions of the 17th, 18th and 19th centuries. There are beautiful gardens and nature trails at this 'pleasant seat'. (Photograph: the author)

Moray and Nairn was owned by the great landholders. With only a tiny electorate and that under the landlords' thumbs, their political dominance was ensured and, until the first tremors of protest in the 1780s, went virtually unchallenged. Henry Dundas, the 'uncrowned king of Scotland', in alliance with landowners like Sir James Grant and the Earl of Findlater and, most powerful of all, the Duke of Gordon and Earl of Fife, chose only MPs prepared to back the Tory government of the day. Even the burghs were dominated by local lairds. In 1784 the burgesses of Nairn complained to the Court of Session that for the previous 30 years their political affairs had been dominated by one family, the Roses. Although the Court decided that the Provost and office-bearers, and the majority of the councillors should be 'residenters' the House of Lords overruled the Scottish judges. Even the Reform Act of 1832, that first faltering measure of political reform, brought little significant change.

Personal rivalries certainly enlivened some of the elections. With a handful of votes either way deciding the issue, some candidates and their backers used strongarm tactics to overwhelm the opposition. This was the case in 1820 when General Duff, who was strongly supported by his relative Lord Fife, was challenged by a candidate backed by Lord Seafield and the Grants of Strathspey. Both factions kidnapped Elgin town councillors to keep them from voting. Then when the Laird of Grant's sisters, who resided at Grant Lodge in Elgin, were seemingly threatened by unruly pro-Fife Elginites, a messenger was despatched to summon assistance from Strathspey. It was Sunday and the tenants, who were at Sabbath worship, were speedily mustered and, like the clan armies of old, were despatched towards Elgin. With pipes skirling, this force of some 600 men marched into the town and headed for Grant Lodge. Although the Duff faction mobilised their supporters, fortunately good sense eventually prevailed and the Grant contingent was withdrawn from Elgin. While the Fife candidate was unsuccessful, the Elgin folk got their revenge by lampooning their opponents.

'Oh, the Grants they are a filthy race,
Have brought themselves into disgrace,
For they made the drums and pipes to play
At Grantown on the Sabbath Day.'

There was a variety of other ways whereby the lairds could demonstrate their social prestige. The most obvious, and often the most essential, was by house improvement. Some owners, as at Ballindalloch, Cawdor, Brodie, Kilravock and Cullen, enlarged old tower-houses. Others asserted their often new-found status by commissioning a new mansion. For example in 1724, William, Lord Braco and first Earl of Fife, built Balvenie House at Dufftown to replace the medieval castle of the same name. Duff House, Lord Braco's even more splendid mansion at Banff, was designed for him by William Adam in baroque classical style. A dispute over costs and fees embittered the relationship between Adam and his client. The ensuing protracted court case, as well as precipitating the architect's death, ensured that the original ambitious plan was not fully

Classical-style Darnaway Castle is surrounded with ornamental park-
lands. The 19th century exterior encloses a remarkable 15th century
great hall. (Photograph: the author)

implemented. So bitter was Lord Braco that, when driving past
Duff House, he averted his eyes and even, it was said, pulled
down the blinds of his coach. The new house was left for his
son to complete. Braco, who was granted an Irish peerage in
1759, preferred to dwell at Balvenie. Ironically while substantial
parts of the ancient stronghold of Balvenie still survive, little
now remains of the early Georgian house.

As we have already noted, estates like Darnaway and
Pitgaveny were embellished by large-scale tree planting. Of
course, property owners like the Earls of Moray also saw
large-scale tree planting as a commercial proposition. On
the other hand, there was no possibility of economic returns
from the ornamental gardens which were very much in
favour. Some old-style formal gardens were refashioned and
landscaped according to the new naturalistic mode of design.
Landowners employed fashionable landscape designers like
Englishman Thomas White who, in the 1780s, worked at
Gordon Castle, Cullen House and Duff House. Some of the
expensively altered gardens were viewed with some disfavour,
however. A visitor to Gordon Castle in 1793 deemed the new
garden to be 'a flat and ill-kept lawn surrounded with thick

plantations and not even commanding a view of the Spey.'
Follies, designed as picturesque adornments, included the
Temple of Fame at Cullen. This rotunda, which stands
close to the main coast road, has recently been restored.
Ornamental estate bridges were another 18th century fashion.
Some impressive works were erected, including Lord Fife's
Brig of Alvah over the Deveron and the Adam-built West
Bridge at Cullen. Craigmin Brig over the Buckie Burn at
Letterfourie in Banffshire is a particularly strange example
of an estate bridge. There are hollow inner spaces in the
centre section of this tiered bridge which were presumably
designed as a weight reducing device. Local legend says
— quite erroneously — that Bonnie Prince Charlie was
concealed there after Culloden. Since Robert Adam designed
nearby Letterfourie House (1773), it is likely that the quaintly
picturesque Craigmin Brig was by him or one of his disciples.

The thrust for prestige took some curious forms. In 1792
the 2nd Earl of Fife built a Gothic-style family mausoleum in
the grounds of Duff House. He then proceeded to instal three
impressive sculptured monuments which were, he claimed,
ancestral relics. One a carved tomb and effigy, which is still
at Duff House, was flitted from St Mary's Church in Banff. The
other relics were removed from the auld kirk of Cullen, with
the consent, it must be said, of the patron, the Earl of Findlater.
The monuments filched from Cullen comprised a stone slab,
incised with the figure of a knight, and a fine carved tomb.
Surmounting the tomb is an intriguing, and indeed rather
mysterious, stone effigy. The purpose of the removal of all
these monuments was to provide the Duffs with a lang, but
regrettably bogus, pedigree. To compound the offence, fake
inscriptions and dates were added. In 1966 the Cullen relics,
fraudulent inscriptions and all, were reinstalled in the kirk from
which they were purloined.

Imposing entrances and gate-lodges also reflected their
proprietors' desire for status and prestige. The Collie Lodge
at Banff was erected in Doric temple form to guard the northern
entrance to Duff House. Today it is used in a way that is the
reverse of its former function. Since it now serves as a Tourist
Information Office, its occupants help visitors to find their way
towards Duff House which has became one of Banff's visitor

Brodie Castle. (Photograph: the author)

attractions. One doubts whether the 2nd Earl of Fife would have approved. In 1765 he authorised his factor to appoint a park-keeper. 'The gates must be kept constantly locked. There is nothing makes the place so disagreeable to me as that constant crowd of idle people that are walking over my grounds when I am at home.' Ballindalloch Castle, built where the River Avon joins the Spey, has a very imposing entrance. The lodge which adjoins the ornamental gateway is a fairy-tale tower-house in miniature. While lairds were erecting castle-like buildings of a purely ornamental nature, genuine medieval strongholds, as at nearby Drumin, were falling into ruin. When it was finally abandoned is unclear, but in 1818 a farmhouse was built by the castle by William Mitchell, factor to the Duke of Gordon. It may be mentioned, in passing, that his predecessor as factor at Drumin was the remarkable William Marshall, who combined technical and mathematical ability, which he employed in astronomy and clock-making, with musical skills as violinist and composer of Strathspeys.

All these estate changes and new buildings were immensely expensive. While money might come in from investments in business enterprises like quarries and new harbours and from the higher rents that could be levied on the improved farms, the costs were still enormous. In consequence, even the very rich could find themselves overextended. Alexander, 4th Duke of Gordon, was notoriously extravagant and heavily in debt. The Earls of Fife, for their part, very wisely refrained from building the wings that were in William Adam's original plan for Duff House. When landowners ran into trouble, they had to look for alternative sources of finance. The 19th Brodie of Brodie had improved and greatly adorned his property, but by the time of his death in 1754 he had impoverished the estate. Despite infusions of cash from sons who made fortunes in India, overspending on grandiose building projects by the 22nd Brodie of Brodie worsened the situation. In addition to further enlarging the house 'in the old English style', he landscaped the flat and naturally 'uninteresting' surrounding land. In 1842 William Ogilvie, schoolmaster at Dyke, described it thus — 'its numerous avenues of noble trees, and an artificial pond, have supplied the place of natural beauty, and make it a delightful residence.' Fortunately for him the then laird, William, had four years earlier found the means whereby he could meet the enormous cost of his improvements. He took the time-honoured way of solving a financial crisis by marrying a rich heiress. Kilravock in Nairnshire was another indebted estate, the consequence, it would seem, of a protracted lawsuit. The 21st laird went out to Bengal in the hope of redeeming the Rose family fortunes. Other male Roses, as with many other members of the landed gentry, opted for a military career.

Wealth from southern industries also brought benefit to the north, with the Morays of Darnaway, for example, enriched by the royalties from their coal-bearing properties in Fife. It was the enormous riches that came, indirectly, from Welsh coal that paid for some of the estate improvements at Pluscarden. The Bute family owned Cardiff Docks and the dues paid on the huge quantities of coal exported from that port went towards their many building projects which included repair work on the ruined Abbey of Pluscarden. That ancient property was purchased from the Duke of Fife in 1898 by the third Marquess of Bute who, as a Roman Catholic convert, was an enthusiastic medievalist. In addition to reviving Pluscarden as a Catholic place of worship, Lord Bute also restored the former Franciscan friary at Elgin.

New money made from trade was also invested in stone and lime and estate improvement. After James Brander, a Moray loon, had made his pile in Lisbon, he returned home and purchased in 1765 the estate of Pitgaveny where he built an imposing classical-style mansion. His brother, Alexander, had also been a merchant but in London and likewise wished to become a country gentleman. On his return, he too bought lands in his native shire. While they were obviously seeking social status, the brothers were also out to increase the value of their property and to this end drained a large part of Loch Spynie. This, though, aroused the ire of Sir William Gordon, the Laird of Gordonstoun, and the resulting quarrel resulted in a costly legal dispute. It was a later Brander, who built Branderburgh and the new harbour at Lossiemouth.

Although the landowners were, and had to be, the initiators in the early stages of agrarian improvement, in the next phase it was the pace-setting tenant-farmers who took the lead. The clergymen, who wrote the parish reports for the New Statistical Account of 1845, highlighted their achievements. In Boyndie, although the support of the Seafield family was acknowledged, the parish minister praised the endeavours of specific farmers. Their improvements had included the reclamation of waste land, installing sub-soil drainage systems, clearing away obstructive rocks and stones, and making greater use of bone-meal and other fertilisers. In nearby Gamrie, the minister highlighted the accumulative effect of the changes wrought by the tenant of Greenskains. This farmer, a Mr Graham, had started to use bone-meal in 1829 and this produced fine crops of turnips and other produce. With a plentiful supply of neeps he was able to keep more cattle over the winter. This meant more dung, which went back on the land thus further increasing its fertility. The installation in 1834 of tile-drains, for sub-soil draining, was an expensive business. As, however, good arable land doubled in value, this was, in farmer Graham's view, 'the greatest of our modern improvements'. Greenskains, as in many other north-east farms, benefited too from the new breeds of cattle, sheep and other livestock that were then gaining favour. In Edenkillie in Moray one tenant farmer, an Alexander Wilson, made such a mark that one of the proprietors erected a marble tablet in the local kirkyard to commemorate 'his zeal and fidelity' as an improver. Elsewhere in Moray progress was being made. According to the Birnie minister, selective cross-breeding had greatly improved the cattle-stock. The pioneers there had introduced Cheviot sheep and shepherds, from the Borders, to look after them.

All these herds and flocks had to be fed, of course. As practical farmers like Mr Graham of Greenskains recognised, the humble neep was the key to this particular rural revolution. 'If there were any justice,' John R. Allan observed, 'the turnip would have a statue in its honour in every market town of the north.' The craze for new, neep-fattened breeds had its downside, however, as the old breeds of livestock were virtually wiped out. The old Scotch sheep, for instance, was virtually extinct by the mid-19th century. Today, Soay sheep (to be seen at Leith Hall in Aberdeenshire) or North Ronaldsay sheep would be the nearest equivalents to the rangy old Scotch Dunface, with its brown face and legs, short wool and wide-spreading horns.

Improvements in transport helped to repay those stock-breeders who had paid good cash for their Cheviot sheep and for cattle, like the Shorthorn and Aberdeen-Angus breeds that were developed in the course of the 19th century. Cattle formerly sent 'on the hoof' to southern trysts were from 1847 being despatched direct to the London market by steamboat. As ship-borne livestock arrived in better condition, they fetched far higher prices. Later, the extension of the railways permitted even speedier shipments of cattle, sent latterly more in the form of 'dead meat'. Although the prosperity thus engendered did not survive the century, the fatstock producers of the north-east withstood the years of agricultural depression better than the grain-producers of the south.

By the mid-19th century many of the farm buildings in the lowland areas at least had been transformed. The substantial stone-built farm-houses built for the larger holdings show that for the lairds and well-doing tenant farmers this was indeed a time of confident expectation. The new farm steadings with their cart-sheds, byres, granaries and other purpose-built buildings were another indication of the considerable amount of capital that was invested in agriculture in this age of High Farming. In some cases, as with some farms in the parish of

Hungryhills Farm near Banff. Is the name meant to convey a message? (Photograph: the author)

Alves, the new buildings were erected by the tenants, with the proviso that, on the expiry of the lease, they could claim financial compensation from the landlord. For the small holders and crofters, particularly in the upland areas, the lesser returns from marginal lands meant that they paid much smaller rents, so the landowners built for this class of farmers a much simpler style of dwelling and steading.

Less immediately obvious but no less important relics of this period of land-clearance and enclosures are the drystane dykes that criss-cross the landscape. The stones used to build the dykes were often cleared from the fields that they enclosed by a great deal of back-breaking labour. When the fields, or parks in the auld usage, were cleared of boulders and stones, subsoil drains, as already mentioned, could be installed. Tileworks were built to meet the demand for drainage tiles. One such works at Blackpots by Whitehills survived until the late 1970s. The drainage tiles manufactured at this regrettably demolished industrial monument and others of the same nature helped change the agrarian landscape. Underground tile drains enabled farmers to level off fields that once been deeply ridged.

The rigs of the old runrig, or ridge and furrow, method of cultivation were ploughed flat, thus permitting more and larger machines to be employed. Here and there the old outfield rigs can still be discerned, last ploughed most likely in the days of open fields and multiple-tenancy ferm-touns. Where such traces of runrig survive, it is generally on poorer ground that was used for pasture and thus escaped the intensive cultivation of the High Farming era.

Not everyone succeeded. For some farmers new buildings proved to be expensive liabilities particularly when there was an economic downturn. Lower prices in 1802–3 seemed to have had deleterious consequences in some areas. Writing in 1842, the Rev Dr Richard Rose of Drainie condemned the landlords of that time for their lack of discernment in their choice of tenants for their new, enlarged farms. These tenants had swept away the 'old butts and bens, with kitchen and spens [inner room]'. In their 'folly and extravagance', they had erected instead 'mansions with dining rooms, drawing-rooms, and parlours, which they could not furnish, or afford to furnish . . .'

The enlarged farms of the high farming time brought new prosperity to many north-east farmers. Those with social aspirations no longer welcomed labourers into the kitchen for an evening meal. As the bothy ballad 'The Weary Farmers' makes only too evident, the farm servants on their part resented the airs and graces put on by some masters and mistresses.

'On cauld kail and tawties
They'll feed ye up like pigs,
While they sit at their tea and toast,
Or ride into their gigs.
The mistress must get "Mem" — and ye
Maun lift yer cap to her;
And ere ye find an entrance
The master must get "Sir".'

CHAPTER 7

Social and Economic Change in Town and Country

'All the carriers, and many of the smaller farmers in the vicinity of Aberdeen, were employed for 10 or 12 days before the market: they travelled in caravans, from a dozen to 40 together; their approach was announced with joy, when first decried upon the brow of the distant hill — "There comes summer eve, and the foremost troop of the packers." '

With these words the folk of the auld village of Keith greeted the travelling merchants who flooded into their village at the time of their Summereve Fair. (The name may be a corruption of St Maelrubha's or St Maury's Fair.) The heyday of this fair was apparently the early 18th century when merchants from as far away as Glasgow, Perth and Dundee were met by their counterparts from the Highlands and 'from the distance even of Kirkwall and the Orkney Isles'. In those days before the '45, the roads were little better than tracks and goods were transported by packhorse. Space had to be found for all the merchandise that was brought in and, an even greater problem, room found for several thousand black cattle and an equivalent number of horses. From the perspective of the more sophisticated 1790s, the Rev William Leslie was amazed at how such a vast throng of people and huge quantities of goods could have been lodged in such a little place.

'Male and female . . . lay together in dozens and scores upon straw, with blankets, in all the pantries, barns, and kilns of the town, and of the farms, to the distance of miles around: — such was then the simplicity of manners!'

Although, by the end of the 18th century, it was still regarded as the most important fair in the north for black cattle and horses, Summereve's great days were over. Certainly linen cloth, farm equipment and other items were on sale at Keith and other fairs. But by then the fairground merchants had to face competition from other retailers. There were, for instance, far more shops. From the Old Statistical Account for Rathven

The Auld Brig o Keith: this crossing-place on the River Isla helps to explain Keith's early importance as a trysting centre. (Photograph: the author)

we learn that — 'Five and forty years ago there was not a single shop, nor any imported article for sale in the parish. About the year 1750, the first shop was opened in Buckie . . ; at present there are 8 merchants or shop-keepers in it . . .' Since they imported coal, salt and iron as well as exporting fish and grain, they were not just simple shopkeepers. In the county town of Banff, there had been shops but they were of a general nature. By 1798 specialist shops such as grocers, ironmongers, and haberdashers had been established. A variety of luxury goods were available. Genteel Banffers patronised a confectioner, whose appetising wares included apricot jelly and ice-cream, and a perfumer 'who deals in such rare articles, as Neapolitan cream for the face, Persian dentrifice for the teeth, and Asiatic balsam for the hair.' Some clergymen regretted the decline in use of homespun clothing and other local products. In late 18th century Elgin the 44 shops sold 'imported', that is to say, non-local goods. Although the increased demand for tea-kettles and hats was sometimes seen as an indicator of economic progress, the

Rev John McDonnel of Forres conveys a contrary impression. 'About 50 years ago there were only 3 tea-kettles in Forres; at present there are not less than 300. The blue bonnets of Forres were then famous for good credit, and at that period there were only 6 people with hats in the town; now above 400.' The minister went on to comment — 'Happy for our country did we keep pace in virtuous improvement, with the extravagant refinement adopted in dress and manners.'

The same clergyman noticed too how retail practice had changed. In Forres there were 60 merchants and shopkeepers who were 'formerly principally supported by travelling and vending their goods in all the villages and market towns to the west and north, particularly Sutherland, Caithness, and Ross, and as far as Orkney. This trade had by 1795 largely gone as these areas now had 'stationary shopkeepers, who can retail their goods nearly upon as low terms as the merchants of Forres.'

In the poorer areas specialist skills were less in demand usually because they couldn't be paid for. Two incomers, a shoemaker from Edinburgh and a tailor from Dundee, found it impossible to earn a livelihood in the upland fastnesses of Kirkmichael. Lawyers, on the other hand, were more in demand since the locals were prone to litigation. For the Rev John Grant, the somewhat acerbic parish minister, lawyers were vampires. They were to be seen at the two annual fairs held at Tomintoul 'walking in consequential state, attended by their clients, while words sweet as honey from their lips distil. But the honey, in the issue, never fails to change into gall, to some one or other of the contending parties.' In upper Banffshire, as in many other areas, there was then no resident medical practitioner. 'Mountain air, and constant exercise, render their aid, for the most part unnecessary.' At any rate, he bitterly added, 'the people can ill afford to pay doctors and retainers of the law at the same time.'

Losing much of their former economic importance, some of the old-established fairs were abandoned as at Banff where, although the burgh charter permitted seven or eight, only four fairs were held, three of which were feeing markets. Locations, too, were altered. Fairs once held in the kirkyard of Duthil were 'partly discontinued and partly transferred to the village of Grantown.' In Rathven, one of the two annual fairs had been discontinued by 1842. The other one, alternatively known as Peter Fair or Rathven Market, continued for the sale of livestock, particularly horses. At the present time Peter Fair is one of the few fairs that is still on the calendar (at the end of July). Surviving, of course, purely as a funfair, it is a great social occasion for the people of Buckie and district. In the 19th century fairs and annual markets were frequently criticised by the clergy for conducing to drunken and violent behaviour and to sexual immorality. Feeing markets, which were often comparatively new institutions, were roundly condemned by Robert Grant, a Forres advocate. Introduced to the Forres area in the 1830s because the new, large consolidated farms required a steady supply of labour, these farmer-controlled markets were assailed for lowering the moral standards of 'our labouring classes, both males and female.'

In the new farms the accommodation for farm servants was usually extremely poor. In the 19th century, and indeed well into the 20th century, it was commonplace for unmarried labourers to live in a bothy or chaumer. By the standards of the day, the best bothies were reasonable enough quarters. These were, however, the exception. More typically the bothy, as described in 1867, was a single room of moderate size, which was seldom clean — 'a heap of coals will be seen in one corner and of firewood in another; it is furnished with no table and no seats, so that on returning from work the only place which the servants have to sit down upon is their chests.' The worst examples were just sections of stables, with the farm horses on one side of a thin and defective wooden partition and the farm chiels on the other. Even as late as 1918, when a Royal Commission on Housing reported, there were still bothies that were 'not fit to house animals.' Even when its structure was sound, the bothy 'combined a maximum of discomfort with a minimum of civilized conditions.'

Where the men slept in a chaumer, or berrick, they had access to the comparative comfort of the farm kitchen. Unlike the bothy lads, the single men who came to the kitchen in the evening had their meals provided for them and thus were more often under the eye of the farmer and his wife. With this kitchen or kitchie system, although the servant quines were

Bothy men at Blairmaud farm near Banff in 1927. The solitary female is possibly the woman who cleaned for them. (Photograph: Scottish Ethnological Archive)

perhaps also more accessible, the more rumbustious workers preferred the greater liberty and licence of the bothy.

It was not just government investigators who criticised the bothy system but also clergymen and other moralists. Farm workers, females as well as males, had, unlike most of the rest of the rural population, managed to escape the attention and supervision of the local clergy. Their habit of frequent flittings meant that ministers found them difficult to pin down. As 'mere sojourners in a parish, and unknown to minister or people', they were, to the regret of a Boyndie clergyman, 'independent of public opinion'. His counterpart at Alves in Morayshire, writing in 1835, drew attention to the fact that, with regard to illegitimate births, the majority of 'delinquents' in his parish were hired servants. He deprecated the practice whereby farmers hired female servants 'at the public market in Elgin, *without any certificate of character.*' The high rate of illegitimacy in the north-east, later confirmed by census returns, was a continuing source of worry. That Banffshire had the highest rate of all aroused concern and provoked a great deal of sermonising: prayer was the sole remedy according to one clergyman. A great deal of ink was spilt in investigating, and theorising about, the reasons why there were so many illegitimate births among the rural folk, but not the fishers, of Banffshire and other north-eastern counties (and also, it should be said, of the south-west right at the other end of Scotland).

Certainly there was a more relaxed attitude to sexual mores in those areas, or, as academics put it, there was an 'illegitimacy subculture'. For some critics, like William Cramond the Cullen schoolmaster, the bothies and 'what is far worse the farm kitchen system' were major contributory factors. Certainly, Bothy Ballads like 'Eence Upon a Time' convey a similar message. The warning given by the mistress of the place to her servant lass who was 'cook aboot the hoose' had been —

'That I maun be safe in the hoose,
Afore 'twas candlelicht-o.'

But Johnny, her bonnie lad, relishing more than the 'breid an' ale' that she dispensed, took this servant quine 'for his ain'. Although weel contented at the time, she eventually became pregnant or was nabbit, as they used to say.

'Noo Johnny is long since gaen,
And thinks of me nae mair-o,
And I maun seek another lad,
To faither Johnny's bairn-o,

But dinna you think, my bonny lad,
That I am mad about ye,
For I can dae wi' a man,
And I can dae withoot ye.'

While this ballad is undoubtedly cautionary, it also makes clear that the lass was not bereft of all resource. With Johnny long gone from the scene, she was looking for a father for Johnny's bairn. But, in the free-and-easy rural culture of the north-east, a husband (or a wife for that matter) prepared to

take on someone else's child was not necessarily difficult to
find. Having a bastard child was, as one clergyman grudgingly
conceded, not 'a serious bar to marriage: indeed, you would
sometimes think it is a recommendation.' Nor for that matter
was 'a man' absolutely essential. For, as the narrator says to her
'bonny lad', she could take him or do without him. The line —
'And I can dae withoot ye' — is unambiguous.

Some investigators noted the absence of cottages available for
married servants. For Cramond, writing in 1892, the landlords
were at fault. When amalgamating farms and creating larger
farming units, they had demolished croft-houses that would
have provided homes for married men. One exception was
the Countess Dowager of Seafield who had erected cottages
in the parish of Cullen 'like an English village'. Yet, there
were a lot of small holdings in the parish of Marnoch and, in
addition, cheap accommodation was available in the village of
Foggieloan. But that was the parish with the highest illegitimacy
rate in Banffshire — 24.2% over the period 1856–1886. Today
attitudes are very different. The publication of the 1990
illegitimacy rate of 20.8% for Banff and Buchan District caused
no great excitement, compared to the furore aroused by the
lower 15.4% rate in 1855–60 in the old county of Banffshire.

For keen students of religious affairs, the illegitimacy figures
in Victorian Marnoch must have seemed rather curious since
the kirk members of that parish had played a significant role
in the dispute, which led to the Disruption. The Disruption
was a major split in the Church of Scotland which led to the
creation in 1843 of the original Free Church of Scotland and
the establishment thereby of what was virtually an alternative
national Church. In the period of debate and controversy that
preceded the Disruption, one of the high points had been a kirk
dispute at Marnoch. Indeed the stand taken by the parishioners
of Marnoch, 'the stronghold of evangelical life in the district',
was subequently highlighted in hagiographical histories of the
Free Church of Scotland.

The core of the dispute of Marnoch as in the Church at large
was the question of patronage. Then at Marnoch as in other
Church of Scotland parishes, the appointment of a minister
was the prerogative of the patron who was usually a major
landowner. (Indeed kirk patronages were once regarded as

Artist's impression of the exodus from Old Marnoch Kirk in 1841.

good investments. In 1769 the second Earl of Fife had bought four north-east patronages for £650. As his agent had advised, purchases that extended his influence and power could not be regarded as expensive.)

The Marnoch dispute began in 1837 when the trustees of the 4th Earl of Fife, who was patron of the parish, presented a minister, the Rev John Edwards, whom the congregation did not want. The patron did eventually give way and sought to mollify local opinion by accepting the man that the congregation preferred. Edwards, for his part though, refused to give way and fought his case through the civil and ecclesiastical courts, thus ensuring that the Marnoch case, as it was termed, became a 'cause celebre'. After four years of wrangling, the original nominee, the Rev John Edwards, was installed at the kirk of Marnoch near the village of Aberchirder. Although it was a cold winter day with a lot of snow on the ground, a huge crowd had assembled, far more than the kirk could hold. As the service of induction commenced, virtually the entire congregation picked up their bibles and solemnly left their pews. Although there was a great deal of shouting and hissing and some snowballs were thrown, it was in the main a pacific protest. The congregation's dramatic exodus as they walked out into the snow was described by a sympathetic reporter: 'The deep emotion that prevailed among them was visible in the tears which might be seen trickling down many an old man's cheek, and in the flush, more of sorrow than of anger, that reddened many a younger man's brow.' The division being irreconcilable, the dissenting congregation built a kirk of their own in the village of Foggieloan. After the even larger exodus at the Disruption of 1843, this New Marnoch congregation joined the Free Church of Scotland.

Those, both ministers and members, who left the Auld Kirk in 1843 sacrificed a great deal. At Buckie, where a new chapel — a church extension charge — had been built just 8 years earlier, the minister, the Rev Robert Shanks, and the great majority of the congregation joined the Free Kirk. Although the kirk had been built, and largely paid for by the local population, the Church of Scotland claimed the building. Reluctantly surrendering their kirk, Robert Shanks and his congregation started to build a new place of worship. With fishermen bringing stones in their boats from a quarry near Hopeman, men and women of the congregation helped to carry them from the beach to the building site. It took some years but by 1850 the new kirk was ready. Victorian Buckie was booming, so quite a few new churches were built, including St Peter's Roman Catholic in 1857, a United Presbyterian in 1870, and an Episcopalian in 1876. Then, to replace the original chapel, the Auld Kirk congregation constructed in 1880 a much larger edifice, complete with a thrusting crown-topped high tower. As with the other kirks and public buildings of the period, this striking edifice, which is prominently located in the main square, symbolised both the prosperity and the kirk-focused godliness of the community: with its Free Kirk rival just up the street, it was a pointed demonstration of the recovery in both morale and numbers that the Church of Scotland had made since the Disruption of 1843. When differences were eventually reconciled and the Free and Auld Kirks were reunited in 1929, this church became Buckie North. Auld loyalties, though, died hard and for long the names of Auld kirk and Free kirk continued in common parlance.

The evangelical revival of 1859 had a considerable impact on Buckie and the other east coast fishing communities. The mainspring in this 'awakening' was a Peterhead cooper and Methodist lay preacher, James Turner, who toured the north-east and preached to large and enthusiastic, and sometimes emotionally excited, audiences. While his mission with its fervid and emotive content led to a revival of Methodism, Turner strongly influenced other denominations. As with other revivals it was a time of uncertainty and anxiety. The fishing had done badly and people were praying for help.

Dressing and parading a burryman was an alternative method employed in those days to bring good luck to the community. When the fishing failed at Buckie, a cooper was dressed in a flannel shirt with burrs (from the burdock plant) stuck all over it. The burryman, who was presumably regarded as a scapegoat figure, was then paraded through the town on a hand barrow. As the religious and moral codes of the fishing community were tightened, this picturesque rite fell into disuse. The last recorded instance of this ceremony in the north-east was at Fraserburgh in 1864. Further south at South Queensferry the tradition is maintained when every year, on the second Friday of August, a burryman is paraded through the town.

From the 1870s onward they could have done with a burryman to bring luck to the rural communities. The prosperity of the high farming era disappeared like, as they said, sna aff a dyke. Improved means of transport meant that grain and other produce from the newly opened-up American prairies and other overseas territories were now being sold on the British market at very low prices. The following years were therefore difficult times for British agriculture. The thrifty farmers of the north-east, where family farms were still common, tightened their belts. The continuing demand for high quality beef, for seed tatties and dairy produce provided lifelines for some. In the upland glens and other areas of marginal land where good soil was scarce, the struggle for farmers working a sma placie was even harder, especially as opportunities for part-time work diminished. Their forebears may have managed to scratch a meagre livelihood from the roch (rough) ground they had cleared by backbreaking toil. But many now were forced to give up the fight. Accordingly, many hard-won upland crofts and small-holdings were abandoned and went back to waste.

While on the larger places increased mechanisation helped cut costs, the consequence was a decreased demand for labourers. A labour surplus, partly alleviated by emigration, meant that tight-fisted employers were able to screw down wages and pour scorn on demands for better conditions and more time for leisure. As this 1887 newspaper extract indicates, the ploughmen at Elgin feeing market were in a poor bargaining position.

'The weather was raw and cold, but altogether favourable for the market, and the attendance both of servants and masters was very large. Business was, however, very stiff, and the supply of labour was much in excess of the demand. Wages generally showed a decrease from last market of from 10s upwards . . . Women were generally getting good wages, and a goodly number attended the market.'

We can imagine the situation. On the one hand, there would have been raw lads anxiously seeking their first fee and, on the other, skilled horsemen weel acquainted with the Horseman's Word which may have given them the trick of handling beasts, but was no magic password to finding employment when times were hard. If the women were being offered better terms than usual, there must have been mill-work or other alternative forms of employment available which helped to keep their wages up.

The Great War (1914–18) brought temporary respite. Real prosperity on a long-term basis returned only when the outbreak of the Second World War in 1939 brought increased demand once more. The post-war period was another time of far-reaching change. This account, written in 1952, describing the changes seen in the Nairnshire parish of Ardclach is typical of the time.

'During the past 25 years agricultural methods have been revolutionised by the introduction of the tractor. At the time of the 'Old Statistical Account', (1792) there were about 300 horses in the parish, now there are only 30 and this number is rapidly decreasing. With the aid of the tractor fewer hands can do more work in less time. The first combine-harvester was introduced during last year's harvest (1951) . . . Thus, within living memory, from the time when crops were reaped

A Banffshire hill-croft. Note the once ubiquitous Ferguson tractor. (Photograph: the author)

by heuk and scythe, and threshed by flail or hand-driven mill a great change has been effected. Great changes have also taken place in regard to farm service. Feeing markets are now but a memory, and masters and servants make their own private arrangements based on a standard rate of pay, but without the old-time perquisites, such as oatmeal, milk, potatoes and coal. As well as having an annual week's holiday with pay, farm servants now work a 48 hour week, compared with the 60 hour week of 30 years ago; even with the shorter working day, the farm servant also has a "mid-yoken" break when he partakes of a flask of tea and a "piece". Unlike his predecessor, he is free when his day's work is over, since there are seldom horses to feed and groom or stables to clean. Many own motor cycles, and some even cars, and are thus able to get away from home during week-ends.'

With post-war subsidies and in more recent years European Community grants, the farming community returned once more to a measure of prosperity. But many craftsmen and other specialised workers have virtually vanished. Gone are the village or parish blacksmiths, carpenters, millers, shoemakers, tailors, weavers. And the surviving rural shopkeepers too have become very much an endangered species. Increased mechanisation and greater efficiency have reduced the number of farms and also the number of employees required. As always it has been the upland areas that have come off worst. Successive economic blasts have meant that bracken has replaced barley and nettles now grow within the sad, broken walls of the croft-houses of yesteryear.

As for the lairds, the agricultural depression saw many estates change hands. Disputes over wills and inheritance and the expensive tastes of the 4th Earl had already weakened the once 'lucky' Duffs, although, by most other standards, the Duffs were still enormously rich. In other ways, too, their luck still held, when in 1889 the 6th Earl married Princess Louise, daughter of the Prince of Wales, and when ten years later Queen Victoria made the Earl Duke of Fife. In the early 20th century heavy taxation and death duties led to the break-up, however, of many more estates. In the 1930s Gordon Castle at Fochabers, home of the Duffs' erstwhile rivals, was sold to the Commissioners of Crown Lands. The Gordon connection was, though, resumed in 1952 when the castle and policies and lucrative Spey rod fishing rights were purchased by Colonel Charles Gordon-Lennox, a cousin of the then Duke of Richmond and Gordon. Although most of this once enormous ducal palace has been demolished, Gordon Castle is still a substantial edifice.

Gordon Castle is today rather unusual inasmuch as it has not been opened to the public. Quite a few of the other big hooses, if not demolished or converted to other uses, are now open to visitors. In more dangerous times, the lairds strengthened their castles and towers to keep unwelcome visitors out, and their 18th and 19th century successors erected high walls to keep out the plebs and also planted screening belts of trees to ensure privacy. To make ends meet, the late 20th century owners not only make grounds and gardens available for viewing, but also invite the public at large into their abodes. Thus, a number of lairds have made the transition from, so to speak, fortified tower-hoose to 'Trust' house.

CHAPTER 8

The Fishing Communities

'From the Firth of Dornoch to the Firth of Forth, the coast is
regularly and thickly planted with villages, the male inhabitants of
which are principally occupied in the white fishery . . . Within these
ten or twelve years, by the enterprising spirit of some merchants in
Aberdeen, Peterhead and Banff, the London market has been laid
open . . . which has occasioned a consequent increase of numbers
as well as employment of fishermen.'

Of the villages mentioned in the above extract, which is from
a report of 1786, a large proportion were on the south shore
of the Moray Firth, with a particularly dense concentration
on the Banffshire coast between Portgordon and Macduff.
Apart from salmon, which merits separate consideration, the
marketable catch consisted mainly of white fish. While many of
the villages described above had been 'planted' comparatively
recently, fish and other maritime species had for long been an
invaluable resource. Documentary evidence, however, is scarce.
There are a few odd references: for example, the fishtoun of
Down — renamed Macduff in the 18th century — is mentioned
in a document of 1440. Findhorn, Covesea and Stotfield (now
part of Lossiemouth) were also old settlements: they appear (the
latter as Coisie and Stotfauld) in a map surveyed by Timothy
Pont and Robert Gordon of Straloch and printed in Amsterdam
in 1654 — see map on page 87. The fishermen of Stotfield
are mentioned in kirk session records of 1670 — condemned
for the superstitious and 'idolatrous custom of carrying lighted
torches round their boats on New Year's Eve'.

Other settlements, as we saw in chapter 5, were planned
villages like Portgordon and Hopeman. Government aid and
the new markets mentioned in the above quotation had
evoked a response not just from fish merchants but also
from lairds. Go-ahead proprietors, seeking to create profit-
making enterprises, enticed fishermen from older settlements,
dangling the bait of better facilities. In the early 1800s the
proprietor of Burghead built houses as an inducement to

117

East Harbour, Lossiemouth.   RELIABLE [##] SERIES.

Stotfield harbour at Lossiemouth, opened in 1839, was subsequently extended. The sailing craft include Zulu herring drifters.

'practical fishermen', principally from Ardersier parish to migrate to this Moray Firth village. Even earlier, Portnockie, as we have seen, was started by migrants from nearby Cullen and Findochty by fishers from Fraserburgh.

By the late 18th century most of the east coast fishermen were working full-time and all year long. Many of the boats they used, though, were very small. While the small inshore boats were often owned by the fishermen themselves, the larger vessels which were required for longer expeditions had to be financed by the lairds. Measuring 7 to 9 metres in length, the large-size boats carried a crew of seven. At Buckie, for a large boat, which was the only type used there and which normally lasted for seven years, the lairds paid £11 towards the total outlay of £24. (There was a rather similar arrangement in force at Stotfield and Covesea where the fishermen were in hock to the Laird of Kinnedar.) The fishing community, though, paid a stiff price for their boats. As well as paying a very heavy rent in cash and in kind, the Buckie fishers had to perform services for the laird carrying, for example, building materials including stones from Covesea quarry and timber from Speymouth. Even more onerously, they also had to bind themselves to serve in the boat for the seven years that the agreement ran. The proprietor at Easter Buckie in 1793 was a Mr Baron Gordon and at Nether Buckie (Buckpool) a Mr Dunbar. George Hutcheson, in his 'Days of Yore' (1887), tells us that the Laird of Nether Buckie, when presumably the fishermen were chary about the weather, wielded a big stick to force them to go to sea. Neil Gunn makes reference to this story in 'The Silver Darlings', his classic novel about the herring fishers of Caithness. Hutcheson, who evidently trawled oral sources, tells us that the laird put reluctant fishers into the joogs — i.e. manacled them to a wall. From around 1821 the Buckie fishermen, enriched by the herring boom of the early 1800s, opted out of these one-sided bargains and started to build their own vessels. Elsewhere this system lasted longer. It was still in use at Sandend and Portsoy in 1842.

Although some of the seatowns or fishertouns, as they were variously termed, were part of, or adjuncts to, historic burghs like Nairn, Cullen and Banff, they were virtually distinct communities. In Cullen and Nairn, for example, the fishertouns were physically separate from the burgh proper. Although some did adapt and become fishermen, the countryfolk saw the fishing populace as strangely different and this feeling was reciprocated. The saying — 'He's nae ane o oors' — was a not uncommon expression. At Buckie earlier this century the fishers referred to the non-fishing population as the 'Granders' — a term indicative of the social divisions in the community at large. The business people of the coastal burghs, however, were only too well aware of the economic value of an active fisher populace. In the middle of the last century Banff Town Council induced some Portnockie fishermen to migrate to Banff. While assisting them to build dwelling-houses, the Council balked at the Portnockie families' request for free education for their families.

As to alleged racial differences, this writer considers that stories about fisherfolk having exotically foreign origins belong to the realm of mythology. Originally, fishermen had combined farming and fishing and so were, as long remained the norm in the Highlands and Islands, crofter-fishermen. As fishing became a specialised activity, so differences developed and in time became more accentuated. Inasmuch, therefore, as north-east fisherfolk had a distinctive life style and lived in their own tight-knit villages, it was because of their type of work and the demands of their calling. These differences, it should be said, go back a long way. When in the 1640s the kirk session of Cullen had difficulty in getting the local fishers into church on Sundays, the session required the skippers of the five boats of Cullen's Seatown 'to go in turn Sunday to Sunday and put out the fisher folks in good time to go to divine service.' As late as 1842 the fisherfolk of Whitehills kept to their own gallery when attending Boyndie parish kirk and, rather unusually, their share of the parish poor fund was separately administered. A bemused mutual tolerance ensured that generally fishers and country folk got on well enough. For Banffshire fisherfolk, Summereve Fair at Keith was a great holiday occasion. Three or four families combined to buy a beast which they then drove home. Killed and salted, this 'mart' helped to feed them through the winter. And, of course, the fishwives were familiar visitors to the farms and villages of the rural hinterland.

In the old-style fishing villages, intermarriage within the community was, nevertheless, the rule. If an exception was made, then the other party almost invariably came from a similar village. As the minister of Rathven noted in 1793, the wives and daughters were indispensable. 'The fisher-wives lead a most laborious life. They assist in dragging the boats on the beach, and in launching them. They sometimes, in frosty weather, and at unseasonable hours, carry their husbands on board, and ashore again, to keep them dry. They receive the fish from the boats, carry them . . . to their customers, and to market, at the distance, sometimes of many miles, through bad roads, and in a stormy season.' But that was by no means all. When returning from their fish-selling forays, they foraged for fuel, collecting whins and heather to take home in their creels. Many generations of fishwives also gathered mussels for bait and helped to bait the lines. This latter task, which often involved putting bait on to as many as 1,500 hooks, was shared with other members of the family. Not surprisingly, it was a maxim in the seatouns that 'no man can be a fisher and want a wife.' This wife furthermore had to be someone who had been brought up to the life. Indeed even well into the 20th century the great majority of fishermen, when seeking a marriage partner, still looked to their own, or to a comparable, community. In the mid-19th century her multifarious responsibilities ensured that, as the parish minister of Boyndie wrote in the New Statistical Account, 'the wife occupies a far more important position in the family than in other situations of life.' It was commonplace for the wife to have complete charge of the family finances — for her to be, as was commonly said, chancellor of the family exchequer.

Traditionally the staple catch of the east coast fishers had been white fish. In spring and summer they had gone on long trips, fishing with 'great lines' for cod, ling, halibut and skate. In the winter months, when weather allowed, they fished, generally using the smaller inshore boats, for haddock, whiting and codling. To dispose of their dried white fish, Buckie crews sailed to Leith and even as far as Glasgow and Northern Ireland. Fish livers were sold to make lamp oil. Again, the fishermen were their own agents, sailing to Inverness and other places to dispose of this valuable byproduct. Before the late 18th century, the herring fishery, until then virtually a Dutch monopoly, had been comparatively unimportant. Thanks, however, to organisational improvements on shore, Scottish fishermen began to fish for herring on a systematic basis. Each summer the fishermen of Banff, Moray and Nairn sailed to Wick for the summer herring season and gained thereby more hard cash in their hands than they had seen before. When the fishing was good, crews could earn as much in six weeks as for the whole of the rest of the year. From about 1815 the herring fishery on the south side of the Firth was developed in similar fashion, with a new merchant class handling the commercial side of the operation.

This 'new' fishery had far-reaching consequences. In Nairn, for example, in 1842 the 'fishing town' had increased in size as a result of 'the prosperity attending the herring fishing . . .' Each summer around 200 men and boys, which was the entire male population of the Seaton, sailed to the Caithness coast 'where they remain for six weeks, and on average bring home from £50 to £100 each man, which constitutes a great source of wealth to the town.' All along the coast similar gains were recorded, although catches, and therefore incomes, fluctuated

Gutting herring at Wick.

wildly. At Whitehills the fisherfolk were not only better dressed, but their houses and furniture were 'quite superior to what their forefathers enjoyed.' Although the Caithness fisheries declined, the Moray coast fishermen pursued the herring shoals both locally and further afield, operating over a longer period of time. Local landings meant employment for shore-workers. At Boyndie in 1842 for each herring-boat landing, one cooper and three women were employed, the latter being engaged by the curers as gutters and packers.

The more venturesome seamen sailed long distances. In high summer a few crews sailed to the west coast, seeking the 'big fish'. In 1839, contrasting the industry of the fishermen of Banffshire with the 'apathy' of the locals, a Highland tacksman, giving evidence to a parliamentary committee, praised the efforts of a Buckie crew who in the previous year had spent six very profitable weeks fishing at Lochinver. That crew, like others of the time, would have been sailing in an undecked vessel. From 1860 or thereabouts, however, open boats were replaced by decked or half-decked craft. The more successful catchers ploughed back their profits, building new and larger vessels. One particularly successful type of vessel was the 'Zulu' which took its name from the Zulu War, which was being fought in South Africa in 1879, when the first Zulu was launched at Lossiemouth. This first boat, the appropriately named 'Nonsuch', combined the vertical stem of the extremely seaworthy 'Fifie' and the raking stern of the 'Scaffie', which till the Zulu took over had been the favourite boat of the north-east men. A typical Zulu of the 1890s was carvel-built, with a length of 20 metres and breadth of 5.8 metres, and was extremely fast. These boats, as with their precursors, were owned by the fishermen themselves, either on a share basis or as a family concern.

The gear, including nets, required for herring fishing also involved heavy expenditure and could cost nearly half as much as the boat itself. As with the boat the nets were purchased on a share system. The drifters (so called from the drift nets that were employed) followed the shoals of herring round the coast. Enterprising 'east coasters', with their superior boats, equipment and skills honed over many years, took the lead in developments elsewhere. In the spring the 'east coasters' headed west towards the Minch, and then sailed northward to Orkney and Shetland. Pursuing the shoals down the east coast of Scotland, the crews generally concluded by casting their nets off East Anglia. Yarmouth and Lowestoft were the landing ports for the herring caught at the once prolific Dogger Bank.

The seasonal migrations of the drifter men involved the womenfolk also. Like the boat-crews, the quines or girls followed the herring from port to port. While some went just to the major herring fishings, others, whose sole livelihood it was, travelled widely, even as far as the Isle of Man and Ireland. In the Edwardian heyday, some 60 to 80 girls went from Nairn alone to the principal fishings of Shetland and Yarmouth. While some quines came straight from school, others had been gutters or packers for many decades. In early summer they might be gutting in Shetland or Orkney; then after a spell at Fraserburgh or Peterhead, they followed the southward trail of the drifters. They followed the herring catchers to North Shields or Scarborough and thence to Yarmouth or Lowestoft. Since 'Scotch Fishing Girls' (some of whom were from the east coast ports, others from the Highlands) were a popular subject for photographers, the fisher quines featured on many of the postcards sent from those fishing ports that were also major holiday resorts.

Like the men too, the fisher girls worked in crews. There were three in each crew, two gutters and a packer. When the herring was landed, the girls kept on working until every herring had been gutted, salted, graded and packed into barrels. Gutting 60 to 70 fish a minute was both arduous and dangerous. Despite tying cloth to their fingers for protection, the quines had to endure many an accidental cut. Since the herring were soaked in brine, even tiny cuts caused agony as they were so difficult to heal. Working too in open curing yards in all kinds of weather, the fisher quines truly earned their meagre remuneration. Not that they didn't stand up for themselves! The gutting quines could, and did, assert themselves with short but sudden strikes. As one militant quine testified with regard to a successful strike at Yarmouth in 1936: 'The curers just keepit ye doon and doon, until ye grew that you'd to fecht for yourself.'

Despite the hard and difficult work they faced, when the quines departed for the gutting, they were in holiday mood. The work gave them a sense of independence and a break from their very considerable chores in households where the men and boys were very much 'the Lords of Creation'. For young girls away from home for the first time the absence of the usual restraints was an eyeopener. Describing life in the huts at Baltasound in Shetland, one veteran related to Paul Thompson of Essex University — 'But the Wick women — oh! what a time they had! Ach, a the men was aboot . . . We finished our education, eh? Ach, it's true — what we didna ken, we learnt then!' Although the Yarmouth landladies usually kept an eye on their lodgers who were crammed in often three to a bed and six to a room, that resort with its music halls and other places of mass entertainment was a revelation. Once the special trains carrying the girls reached home in early December, there were presents to distribute. Most fisher homes displayed souvenirs of the 'A present from Yarmouth' type. Not a few of them are up for sale once more — not this time in the souvenir stores but in the antique shops of the area.

Harbour enlargement, as we have noted elsewhere, was of crucial importance, the more especially as bigger boats were

The crew of a Buckie-registered steam drifter 'Girl Lily'. The boatbuilder was William Geddes, Portgordon.

being built for crews who were pursuing the herring into distant waters. This surge in construction meant that fishing touns like Crovie, which had but a small pier, and Sandend, with its tiny harbour, were left behind. The curers too concentrated their efforts in the larger ports. Although the men of the smaller ports were still going to sea, the drifters they owned, or worked in, were based elsewhere.

In the early 1900s the steam drifter further extended the fishermen's range and the length of time spent following the 'silver darlings'. Although a steam drifter was three times more expensive than a sailboat, the herring boat skippers eagerly embraced the new technology. The Buckie area fishers were especially enthusiastic, sinking their savings and taking out mortgages to buy the new catchers. The early 1900s saw indeed a veritable revolution, with in 1913 the Buckie men registering no fewer than 276 steam drifters, which was more than a third of the total Scottish fleet. As with the sailing fleet, members of the crew (except for the engineman and some hired west coast seamen) usually owned a share, if not in the boat, at least in the nets. But since a steam drifter was much more expensive than a sail boat, landsmen — such as fish salesmen, coal merchants and chandlers — also put money into boats. While during the glory days of the herring fishing the share system undoubtedly fostered cooperative effort, for the many seamen with but a minimal share there were drawbacks which became only too apparent in later, less prosperous times.

The wealth engendered from following the herring created a building boom. In Findochty (Finechty to the locals), where the harbour had been improved in 1882–83, the number of houses was doubled in one decade. Most Findochty folk owned their own homes: by 1918 no fewer than 264 of its 266 families were owner-occupiers. As in the other herring ports, a new style of house was developed. The old type of house, and all along the coast there are many upgraded examples still to be seen, contained just two or three rooms. The dwellings built in the late 19th and early 20th centuries for the more prosperous skipper-owners were not just larger, but, since they were designed to meet the occupational needs of the occupants, they were also functionally planned. They were designed not just to accommodate a family but also to house much of the gear that the family members used when earning their livelihoods. In the old days when boats were comparatively small a lean-to or free-standing shed or old upturned boat sufficed as a store. As boats increased in size and catching capacity, the need for space to store and also to repair drift-nets had become a problem. Since the nets and other gear were family or cooperatively owned, the skipper-owners, like other small-scale businessmen managing a family business, sought a solution that enabled them to keep the boat's gear under their own roof-tree. They therefore, earmarked the upper floor, in whole or in part, as a net store. Not wishing, or not being allowed, to haul nets and other gear through the house, well-doing skippers ensured that the house-plan included a second staircase. This took the form of an outside stair which was built at the back of the house to allow easy access. While nowadays the net-lofts have been converted into living-space, the outside staircases usually remain, a distinctive feature of the east coast townscape.

In the traditional fisher dwelling the most comfortable room was the kitchen-cum-living room. The front room, or parlour, though well furnished and spotlessly clean, was rarely utilised: it was reserved for special occasions like weddings and funerals. The front door likewise was seldom opened, the backdoor being the universal entrance. The exteriors no less than the interiors were, and are, also spick-and-span. Thanks to decorative pointing and the liberal application of glossy oil-paint, the houses of the seafaring communities, particularly along the Banffshire coast, are to this day exceedingly colourful and distinctive.

As in so many other aspects of life the 1914–18 Great War was a turning point. The loss of the old continental markets meant that communities that had done well before the war were now impoverished. 'The war murdered our customers' was a common saying on the coast. Having invested so heavily in steam drifters, Buckie now suffered the consequences. In 1921 there were 600 unemployed fishermen in the town. In the previous year the Buckie district communities had demonstrated in strength in peaceful protest to demand a government subsidy for the herring industry. More than 10,000 people marched along the coast to the braes of Strathlene to the greatest meeting ever held on the Moray Firth 'for peaceful purposes'. The protesters' banners harked back to the sacrifices of the Great War: 'Starvation our reward for services rendered'. While their immediate demand was met, the long-term problem remained unsolved. With insufficient income to buy new boats or gear for other forms of catching, the fishermen kept on chasing the herring, using their now ageing and increasingly uneconomic boats. The early 1930s were an even more desperate time, when deckhands on the surviving drifters toiled hard but couldn't even make a living wage. When Peter Anson, marine artist and social historian, revisited Buckie in 1934, he described a sad place where 'hundreds of families found themselves reduced to absolute poverty.' This 'once, proud independent community' had, like most of the other Moray Firth ports, 'acquired almost the same atmosphere of hopeless despair that one finds in the depressed area of South Wales or County Durham.'

As at other times of economic hardship, some found consolation in religion. The East Anglian herring fishing of 1921 brought another evangelical revival. When the crews and gutters

Steam drifters at Buckie in the interwar years. Jones' slip and shipyard is in the background.

reached their home ports, the converts held services, many of them in the open-air, and thus spread the gospel message from port to port. The Salvation Army were influential in this revival and, in consequence, increased their support particularly among the poorer fishermen. James Slater of Portsoy has testified in various writings as to the strength of feeling aroused and the simplicity of the message. 'There was no intellectual nor eloquent oratory, but the word was the testimony of Spirit-filled men, mainly fishermen; and we may remember it was from this type of men the Lord Jesus chose a number of his disciples . . .' Once when fishing out of Portmahomack in the Dornoch Firth, James Slater saw another Portsoy boat approach — 'On meeting fellow fishermen at sea . . . the usual salutation is an enquiry about the fishing: but not this time. Up alongside came the *"Mary Ann"*, and then came a shout from William Jim giving us the names of the converts at the meetings, the fishing was the secondary topic.'

Then, and also in the post-war years, the Aberdeen and Granton trawler fleets gave some opportunities for seafaring work. Another outlet was the Merchant Navy. In January 1938 the Northern Scot, describing the plight of the share fishermen of Burghead, reported that 'during the past year' over fifty of these unemployed men had joined merchant ships. The employment situation was, of course, soon transformed, firstly, by rearmament and preparations for war and then by the actual outbreak of hostilities in 1939.

In the early 1920s, with herring no longer the king of fish, some of the drifter men turned to white fish. A number of the Moray Firth men also experimented with the Danish seine net. Since returns were good, this bag type of net was increasingly employed by the inshore men. Soon the traditional hand lines and other methods of catching were discarded at a number of ports. At Whitehills, for instance, the haddock line had disappeared by 1931. Motor vessels now began to replace the expensively-fuelled steam drifter. With financial backing from shore-based entrepreneurs, the Moray men of the interwar years turned Lossiemouth into the major port for seiners. After 1945, the remaining steam-drifters were one by one discarded: the future lay, it seemed, with diesel-vessels that could be adapted for different types of fishing. As herring became scarce through overfishing, the white fish catching seiners, built with the aid of government grants and loans, predominated. At Nairn, though, the downturn continued. In 1848 Nairn could boast more boats (72) and fishermen (163) than Lossiemouth (54 and 137). During the herring boom the Nairn fishing community (as with Burghead) invested very heavily in the steam drifter. In 1930, even in the time of depression, there were still 263 fishermen in Nairn manning 40 fishing vessels, including 24 steam drifters. But by 1962 there were only 37 full-time fishermen and 6 boats — all motor vessels. In contrast to Lossie, Macduff, and Buckie, Nairn was no longer a significant fishing community.

Unlike Nairn, Buckie recovered and emerged from the doldrums, becoming by 1957 the principal white fish port in the Moray Firth. From the 1950s, too, there were spectacular developments in other forms of fishing. While some species of shellfish, crabs and most of all lobsters, were always valued, the smaller Norway lobster, on the other hand, was once regarded as a nuisance and thrown overboard again. The popular demand for scampi and prawns in various forms has led to

an enormous increase in demand, which demand was met by
adapting boats for light trawling. Not surprisingly, the value of
the shellfish catch, particularly of Norway lobsters, also soared.
By the late 1960s, too, drift netting had been abandoned.

In 1988 there were 54 boats in the Lossiemouth fleet and
nearly twice as many in the Buckie one. These fleets, it should
be said, include vessels which may be owned and crewed by
men from smaller, satellite ports like, say, Hopeman and
Portnockie. Like the driftermen of old, the fishermen of today
are enterprising and innovative. The larger boats, which are
powerful multi-purpose vessels, range very widely and hunt
many different species. When catching off the east coast, they
very often land at Peterhead and, when in northern and
western waters, their land base will be a west coast port such
as Lochinver or Kinlochbervie. It is common practice, though,
for the crews to tie up at a west coast port for a weekend and
travel back to their home port by motor transport.

The change-over from herring drift net to seine net fishing
and the end of line fishing brought social consequences. The
parish minister of Drainie, noting that the women were taking
no part in fishermen's work, wrote in 1953: 'The fish when
landed is sold immediately at the fish market, all the work
having been done previously on board by the men while at
sea. Thus, within the last 25 years one has seen the total
extinction of the "fish-wife". Consequently, a fisherman now
can and does marry outwith his immediate circle, and his
house no longer requires a storage room for nets and gear
but is like any other home . . . The fisherman's wife of today
is a lady of leisure compared to a generation ago.' Gone too
are the former superstitious beliefs and practices, which were
once a feature of these close-knit and clannish communities.
Although as late as 1951 the fishers of Whitehills were still
turning the boat 'with the sun', the old superstitions had
largely died out by then. These beliefs and other aspects of the
changing social scene and, of course too, the story of boats and
catching techniques are ably presented at a number of maritime
heritage centres. There are valuable displays at, among other
places, Lossiemouth and Buckie and not least at the Nairn
Fishertown Museum. Many of Peter Anson's unique maritime
drawings and water colours are housed at the Buckie centre.

With regard to today's scene, fishing can hardly be regarded as a secure way of earning a livelihood. Certainly today's fishing vessels are fitted with electronic equipment which detect the shoals much more easily than before. And their catching capacity is truly awesome. Using purse nets, they can scoop up several hundred tons of fish in one trawl. But today, with too many vessels from many different countries plundering the seas, the European Community has put quotas, and other restrictions, on certain popular species like haddock and herring. The restrictions on herring were just in time, as overfishing by seamen of many nations had well nigh obliterated the shoals of the once abundant 'silver darlings'. Yet, at the same time, since their boats and equipment are exceedingly expensive, the fishermen have large loans to repay. As was the case with the steam drifter, the initial expense and high running costs mean that fishermen have an economic incentive to keep on fishing. Yet at the same time they know that they run the risk of destroying the stocks. In this situation there are no easy answers. As in the interwar period there has been a marked decline in the number of boats and fishermen. Consequently, the fishing communities are under threat once again.

When seafarers' livelihoods are threatened, the ancillary workers also feel the draught. For every fisherman at sea it is reckoned that another five jobs are created onshore through seafood processing, boat-building and other forms of servicing. At Buckie, for instance, shellfish processing is a major employer as is boat-building. Boat-building is a prime example of a trade which, generally speaking, has followed the ups and downs of the fishing industry. Spurts of building came, for instance, when the first Zulu and later the steam drifter came into favour. Kingston, which as we have already noted, was at its peak a major centre of the industry. In addition to Kingston's seven shipyards, there was, in the 19th century, at least one yard at each of the other ports. They were small-scale businesses. In 1842 at Cullen, for example, there were three master builders and 22 employees who constructed on average 44 boats each year and, also, the occasional ship — five ships in all over the previous three years.

In times of poor trade in the fishing industry the north-east boat builders diversified. During the two world wars their

Banff-registered fish catchers at Whitehills. The Saltire flag is prominently displayed on BF 156. (Photograph: the author)

services had been sought by the Admiralty. In the 1950s too the Buckie yards built for the Royal Navy inshore and coastal minesweepers. For countering magnetic mines some of these craft were constructed of aluminium and others of laminated timber. More traditional-style yachts and other pleasure boats have also been built. On one notable occasion in 1971 a three-masted schooner was launched. This was the 'Captain Scott', which was then Britain's largest functioning sailing ship. (This splendid sail training ship was later sold to Oman.) With demand for traditional wooden-hulled craft declining, steel vessels have also been constructed. The Buckie and Macduff boat-builders and marine engineers have, however, been obliged to use south-built hulls.

While stronger and better-equipped, modern fishing craft are by no means immune to disaster. The risks are still there as a visit to the Seamen's Memorial chapel at Buckie makes only too plain. The names of the many local seamen lost at sea since 1945, and significantly too their boats' names, are poignantly listed in this attractive small shrine. The stained glass memorial windows illustrate in symbolic form the life and work and the strength of faith of this historic fishing community. In close-knit communities calamities strike deep and remain in the collective memory for a very long time. The folk of Lossiemouth, for instance, had good reason to remember the Stotfield disaster, when on the 25th of December 1806 no fewer than four boats were lost. The 21 seamen drowned comprised virtually the entire seafaring population of the settlement. But today as in the past the seamen of the north-east are ready to face the difficulties and hardships of a hazardous calling. As Richard Murray concluded when writing about the fishing industry in the 'Third Statistical Account' for Moray and Nairn:

'But while there are fish in the restless Firth, the fishers will launch out.'

CHAPTER 9

The Transport Revolution

'Those who are born to railroads, or even to modern mail-coaches, can scarcely be made to understand how we, of the previous age, got on. The state of the roads may be judged of from two or three facts. There was no bridge across the Tay at Dunkeld, or over the Spey at Fochabers, or over the Findhorn at Forres, nothing but wretched, pierless ferries, let to poor cottars, who rowed, or hauled, or pushed a crazy boat across, or more commonly got their wives to do it . . . To reach Inverness by the mail thirty or even twenty-five years ago took only nine hours short of the time required to get to London.'

Lord Cockburn, writing in 1847, was very conscious of the advances made during his lifetime in transport and communications. Travel and the movement or goods was, as he indicated, a much more laborious business before the age of steam. In addition to poor roads, rivers and difficult burns were major impediments, especially when in spate. With unexplained drowning accidents, it is no wonder that in folklore there were many stories about malevolent water-kelpies. Appearing before stranded wayfarers in the form of a ready-saddled pony, the water kelpy, legend said, plunged its hapless rider into river or loch and a watery grave. Even the provision of a boat was no guarantee of safety. When the ferry boat over the Findhorn at Forres capsized in 1782, thirteen people were drowned.

On the major rivers there were numerous ferry points, as indicated by the frequent use of 'Boat' place-names. Boat of Garten is a well known example. Another historic Spey crossing-place is Boat o Brig near Rothes which name is not so contradictory as it seems: the ferry which plied here replaced a bridge which had been destroyed. As far back as the 13th century, there was a bridge across the Spey at this point and a hospice too for travellers on the eastern side. We don't know when and how the medieval bridge came to be removed or lost, but old farm names like Bridgeton and Briglands outlasted its destruction. When a suspension bridge was erected in the 1830s, the boat went out of use but once

12. Ferry at Blacksboat.

Ferry at Blacksboat on the Spey which was in use till a bridge was built in 1908.

again place-name conservatism ensured that the name survived. Elsewhere, Aberlour for instance, where there was need and at least some local demand, a ferry boat continued until well into the 20th century.

The fact that the Isla was one of the few rivers that was bridged probably helps to explain the growth of Keith as a market centre. The Auld Brig o Keith, which dates back to 1609, is the oldest surviving bridge in the area. In the 18th century, the military imperatives of the British state saw a number of bridges built on the line of new military roads. These were designed to give government troops quick access to strategic locations, thus allowing them to control dissident Highland clans. Dulsie Bridge across the Findhorn is a spectacular example of the military bridges built for Major Caulfeild who was General Wade's successor as Inspector of Roads and Communications in the Highlands. Completed in 1755, this bridge across the Findhorn was an important link on the military road which ran from Coupar Angus in Perthshire to Fort George near Inverness. Traversing, in intimidating

Exceptionally heavy rain caused the rivers to flood in 1829. The floods and consequent damage were on an unprecedented scale. Fishing boats from Findhorn village saved many lives. The illustration, showing a marooned family at Broom of Moy Ferry on the Findhorn near Forres, is taken from Sir Thomas Dick Lauder's *Moray Floods* (1829).

fashion, Jacobite heartlands, the stretch from Braemar to Tomintoul went via Cockbridge and the Lecht which at 644 metres is the second highest road in the country. Going over the Lecht, a route which frequently features in the winter weather bulletins, the military road followed the line of an old track. At the Well of Lecht a stone commemorates the achievement of the five companies of the 33rd Regiment who built the section from there to the Spey.

By the 1790s, however, the military roads had deteriorated and were badly in need of repair. Inadequate river crossings too meant delays and bottlenecks. The inhabitants of Nairn complained that the old bridge over the river of the same name was defective and was needing to be replaced. Improving farmers in Morayshire pointed also to the need for a bridge over the Spey at Fochabers. Their prosperity depended on the easy movement of cattle to and from markets and on the use of large quantities of lime which had to be brought across the Spey from Strathisla in Banffshire.

'Numberless travellers . . . from every part of Britain pass this way,' stressed the minister of Bellie, 'who are frequently detained by floods and boisterous winds, and sometimes cross with danger. The post-boy is, at times, detained, though they raft him over when they would not run the risk with any other person.' The growth in trade and commerce had led to a surge in demand for postal communications. By 1791 the postal revenue at Keith had increased by a hundred fold 'within these 30 years' and the service, with runners bringing the letters from Fochabers just three times a week, was detrimental to 'the increasing trade of the place'.

Gradually though roads and communications were improved, some entirely thanks to local endeavour and others, in part at least, through government grants. Highland distress and the rise in emigration from the north, which threatened to deprive the state of a ready supply of military and naval manpower, led the government to set up a Parliamentary Commission to fund and supervise the construction of roads and bridges in the Highlands. As their consultant in charge of construction, the Commission chose the former Dumfriesshire stonemason and by then experienced and eminent engineer, Thomas Telford. Although outwith the Commission's remit, the task of bridging the Spey at Fochabers did receive a special grant to supplement funds raised by local proprietors. Completed by 1804, the Fochabers bridge was badly damaged in the great flood of 1829. When two of the arches collapsed, two men who had been watching the stupendous flood from the bridge barely escaped. A third, the lame son of Widow Anderson, the tollkeeper, was drowned. The missing span of this toll bridge was replaced first by a wooden arch and subsequently by a cast-iron one. Although bypassed by the modern road, this composite bridge and its tollhouse have survived subsequent floods. Further up the Spey, the Telford-designed iron arch at Craigellachie, like the older Dulsie Bridge, had been raised high enough to escape irreparable damage. As with the Fochabers bridge, the cost of Telford's Craigellachie masterpiece was shared between local subscribers, on the one hand, and the Commissioners for Roads and Bridges, on the other. The ironwork for this remarkable piece of work, which was completed in 1814, came from Wales, having been shipped to Kingston and then carted overland to the site. In 1836 the parish minister at Aberlour stated that the benefits from this toll-free bridge included 'opening up a communication to the Elgin markets, and to Garmouth, the chief grain market for this quarter; from which place too, this part of the country is most conveniently supplied with coals. This grand and picturesquely situated bridge was,' he continued. 'frequently visited by strangers as an object of curiosity.'

From around 1800 many of the main highways were converted into turnpikes. The tolls charged on these pay-as-you-go roads helped to pay for their construction and upkeep. Although locals frequently took exception to, and tried to avoid the toll-charges, the improved roads and new bridges meant that stage-coach services could be introduced. The first stage-coach between Perth and Inverness started in 1806. Five years later a service was commenced which linked Aberdeen to Inverness. The coach on the inaugural run carried six passengers inside and it was hauled by six horses. But this kind of service was not maintained. Lord Cockburn's experience was rather different. The mail-coach of those days was a two-horse vehicle, which held only three persons, two of them facing forward and the third, according to Cockburn, 'stuck into a kind of sentry-box opposite, with his back to the horses, and of course there were no front windows.' The rather antiquated pair of horses which drew this odd-looking vehicle on the stage from Elgin to Forres were locally known as 'the deaf and the blind horse'.

By 1835 standards had been greatly advanced and Elgin, for instance, was served by the 'Star' coach from Inverness. Another went via Banff, and there connected with a stage-coach which went to Aberdeen. The arrival each day of the mail-coach, the 'Mail', aroused great interest, as the postal service had become so efficient that 'a letter despatched from London through the post-office reaches Elgin about three o'clock P.M. of the third day.' Lighter mail-gigs carried the post and, of course, passengers to Lossiemouth and Burghead. There was also the 'Defiance' coach from Edinburgh to Inverness which passed and repassed through Elgin 'in the middle of every

Former kingshouse at Dulsie Bridge. (Photograph: the author)

lawful day' (i.e. excluding Sunday). It was, however, only a comparatively small number of people who could afford to travel by coach. It was a very dear way to travel and, with toll-bars all along the way, the Inverness to Aberdeen route was particularly expensive. As for goods, they went by carriers' waggons. In 1835 there were 'regular carriers to Aberdeen, Banff, and Inverness, and to all the adjacent villages.'

While a few simple hostelries — kingshouses as they were termed — had been established along the line of the military roads, standards generally were low. More travellers very often meant too, space being at a premium, no room at the inn. For reasons of prestige and sometimes, too, their own convenience, some landowners sought to remedy the situation. Inns were built and tenants with new ideas installed. The Earl of Seafield, for example, built in 1822 the Cullen Hotel: later the name was changed to the Seafield Arms. This fine classical-style building is centrally located in the square of the new town of Cullen. It stands next to the old townhall which was built by the Earl at the same time. Although the village contained only 37 families. Tomintoul had by 1793 more than one inn. One of the innkeepers was a Mrs McKenzie, a lady who had led a very colourful life. According to that bitterly-jaundiced scribe, the Rev John Grant, she 'had began her career of celebrity, in the accommodating disposition of an easy virtue, at the age of 14, in the year 1745. That year saw her in a regiment in Flanders — caressing and caressed.' But she rose in the world graduating from camp follower to innkeeper at Grantown. From there that redoubtable lady went to Tomintoul where, keeping the best inn, she now stood in 'personal respect and fortune' at the head of the inhabitants.

Thomas Telford was also involved in harbour improvement and construction which rents from forfeited estates (ie. estates confiscated after the '45), helped to pay for together with locally raised money. In 1819 Robert Southey, poet and friend of Thomas Telford, saw new piers being built at, among other east coast places, Banff and Cullen. Pointing to the value of government aid, he recorded in his journal: 'This whole line of coast is in a state of rapid improvement, private enterprize and public spirit keeping pace with national encouragement, and it with them . . .' Harbour improvements, in the short run at least, brought more trade to the Moray Firth ports. Thanks to more productive forms of fishing and farming, more fish, grain and livestock were exported. From 1826 considerable numbers of live cattle were shipped from Banff to London. Unfortunately the new basin at Banff, built to Telford's design, silted too readily. The problems of clearing it proved too much and Banff's maritime trade fell away. On the other side of the estuary of the River Deveron, its rival prospered as fishermen and traders transfered their allegiance to Macduff where there was a better harbour and also lower charges.

For the Victorians, it was steam locomotion that wrought the greatest changes. A through line from Aberdeen to Inverness was completed by 1858. While the section from Aberdeen to Keith was built by the Great North of Scotland Railway, the stretch from Keith to Nairn was constructed by Inverness entrepreneurs, who three years earlier had completed their own line to Nairn. Bridging the River Spey was a tricky and expensive operation. In 1858 an iron girder span was erected over the Spey at Boat o Brig, Orton. (It was replaced by a steel span in 1906). Although the line which went via Elgin and Keith gave Invernessians a link to the south, it was not the most direct route nor could the Great North be described by any means as accommodating partners. With the experienced Joseph Mitchell as chief engineer, the progenitors of what became in 1865 the Highland Railway embarked on the ambitious task of constructing a line which, going through the Grampian Mountains, would give a link to Perth. A line was led south from Forres across the wind-swept Dava Moor to Grantown reaching that village in 1863. From thence it went to Aviemore and then to the south via the Pass of Drumochter. In 1898 the present, more direct route, from Inverness to Aviemore via the Slochd was opened. But the Forres to Aviemore line provided a useful link from the Moray Firth to the south until its closure in 1965.

Actually the first line in the area was built by the tiny Morayshire Railway Company. The opening in August 1852 of this short six mile long line from Elgin to Lossiemouth was celebrated, as was customary then, with processions, bands playing and general rejoicing. The promoters of this railway, led by the redoubtable Provost Grant of Elgin, had intended to extend into Strathspey. But railway construction in those days was bedevilled by rivalries and differences between the different railway companies. Although the Morayshire Railway people did manage to push their line south to Rothes, that company was forced, albeit reluctantly, into cooperation and then eventual amalgamation with the Great North of Scotland Railway.

Railway fever was epidemic in its effects and a number of small locally-inspired companies were formed. Enjoying varying degrees of success, they were absorbed sooner or later by either the GNOSR or the HR. Branch lines were built which linked the Moray Firth coastal towns to the main lines. One, the Findhorn Railway, was a complete failure. As the harbour silted too easily, the commerce of the port fell away and thus too the railway could not pay and the line, which had opened in 1860, was closed just twenty years later. The Burghead line fared much better, although, while Burghead was connected by 1861, it was another 31 years before the short extension to Hopeman was built. Thanks to the requirements of large maltings at Roseisle and Burghead, the branch-line from the mainline still survives as far as Burghead. The Distillers Company which owns the maltings has its own fleet of ultra-modern waggons.

The Banffshire coast was reached in 1859 when an independent railway was constructed, which linked the fishing and trading ports of Banff and Portsoy to the GNOSR system. The Banffshire Railway, as it was then called, was taken over by the GNOSR in 1867. To exploit the developing whisky distillery traffic, a route was opened between Keith and Dufftown in 1862 and then extended as the Strathspey Railway to Boat of Garten. With the GNOSR given access to the Highland line, the villages and distilleries of Strathspey were well served. There were railway connections to the north and, by way of the Drumochter route, to the south and also to the north-east via the GNOSR. Run in Edwardian times by a comparatively far-sighted management, the Great North started to run buses to outlying villages that were not served by trains. A feeder bus connected Aberchirder in Banffshire to Huntly railway station, and in the summer months a tourist bus ran between Tomintoul and Ballindalloch on the Strathspey line.

Ballindalloch is still an access point for visitors heading south towards Tomintoul, but, since large sections of the now grassed-over old railway tracks have been incorporated into the Speyside Way, many of these latter-day tourists are travelling on foot. This splendid, long distance walking route, which includes a short spur to Dufftown, runs by way of the River Spey, and

Visitor centre for Tamdhu Distillery, on the Speyside Way, is located in the old railway station buildings. Opened as Dalbealie, the name was changed to Knockando in 1905. The line, which was opened in 1863, was closed to passenger traffic in 1965. (Photograph: the author)

some of its tributaries, from Tomintoul in the foothills of the Grampians to the Moray Firth coast. Steam railway buffs are also catered for, as thanks largely to the efforts of railway enthusiasts, the railway track from Boat of Garten to Aviemore was restored in the 1970s. The Strathspey Railway Company run steam trains on this line during the summer and winter holiday seasons. Some tourist excursion trains are also run from Aberdeen to Dufftown, using, on the stretch between Keith and Dufftown, track which had been retained for distillery traffic.

By 1880 the railway companies saw Buckie, with a fast-growing fishing fleet and a new deepwater harbour, as an attractive proposition. While the Great North sought to extend westward from Portsoy towards Buckie and Portgordon, the Highland Railway raised objections and at the same time resuscitated an old plan for a line from Keith. Since both companies' plans aroused considerable argument and contro-versy, the two schemes, and other counter-proposals, were avidly discussed both in the press and at well-attended public

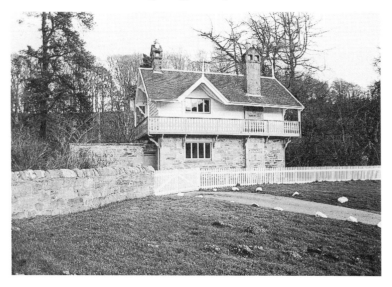

Swiss-style cottage, Ballindalloch. (Photograph: the author)

meetings. In the communities that stood to gain, there was general rejoicing when both companies received the necessary parliamentary approval. At Cullen, as flags were hoisted and bells were rung, the Volunteer Band paraded through the streets, and a celebratory bonfire attracted a vast throng into the town square.

Completed in 1884, the Highland Railway's branch from Keith to Buckie was continued eastward as far as Portessie where a station was shared with the Great North. The rival, Aberdeen-based company completed its coast line in 1886 after building westward from Portsoy to Buckie and thence to Elgin. As the Earl of Seafield, who was on the Board of the Highland Railway, insisted that the GNOSR, keep clear of the grounds of Cullen House, extensive embankments and viaducts had to be built at Cullen. The bridging of the fast-flowing and fickle River Spey at Garmouth was another difficult and thus expensive operation. At the time of construction, the central single span was the longest on any single line bridge in Britain. The Great North subsequently had to face, but successfully countered, a lawsuit from the Duke of Richmond and Gordon

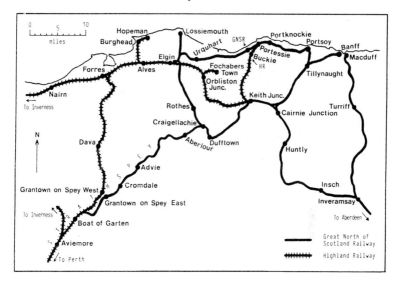

Passenger railways in 1910.

who claimed that the bridge had damaged his salmon fisheries. This Garmouth bridge is now part of a walkway from the village of Garmouth to the Speyside Way. As for the Portessie to Keith line, wartime exigencies (1914–1918) led to the requisition and removal of most of the track. Although the track was replaced by 1925, road vehicles were providing fierce competition for the railways so the Heilan Line, as it was locally known, was never reopened. The story of this fascinating wee railway is related by Brian Wilkinson in his booklet entitled 'The Heilan Line'.

Unlike the Spey, the River Deveron, was not bridged by the GNOSR. That idiosyncratic company preferred, operating through nominally independent companies, to take a separate branch-line to Macduff by way of Fyvie and Turriff. Opened in 1872 the Macduff branch was patronised by fishwives who hawked their fish round the rural parishes. As well as being given a special rate, the fishwives were allowed to transport one loaded creel free of charge. But fish in much larger quantities was despatched to even more distant destinations. In late Victorian days express trains carried fresh fish from Buckie to Liverpool and Manchester in some fourteen hours.

In the heyday of railway growth and development, inland towns like Keith, Elgin and Forres benefited from their focal positions on the railway network. Keith was a key junction in the Great North system as was Forres in the Highland's. In the latter town there were more than a 100 railwaymen. It was the railway engineers who gave their name to the local Highland League Football Club — Forres Mechanics. It was furthermore the extension of the railway network that made league competitions, such as the Highland League, feasible in the first place. As with the fish trade, the cattle trade was also transformed by the advent, in the first place, of the steam ship and, in the second, of the steam train. Improvements in transport helped to repay those stock-breeders who had invested in Cheviot sheep or in cattle like Shorthorns and Aberdeen-Angus, new breeds that had been developed by the mid-19th century. Cattle formerly sent 'on the hoof' were from 1847 being despatched direct to the London market by steamboat. As ship-borne livestock arrived in better condition, they fetched far higher prices. The railways permitted even speedier shipments of cattle, sent latterly more in the form of 'dead meat'. As the new forms of transport virtually put an end to long-distance cattle droving, auction marts were opened at market towns like Elgin, Forres, Keith, Dufftown and Cornhill — all centrally located and all accessible by rail. The following extract from the 'Northern Scot' of 28th April 1888 shows how local businessmen exploited the railway connection. 'Now that Elgin is such an important railway centre we are very pleased to learn that a body of influential local gentlemen are about to form themselves into a company for the erection of a mart in Elgin . . . for the sale of cattle, sheep and horses.' Significantly, the chosen site was close to both the Highland and Great North railway stations.

The arrival of the railways certainly boosted industrial and commercial development in Elgin. And the transfer, in the course of this century, of traffic to the roads has not diminished this growth. As an administrative and commercial centre, the Elgin of today provides employment for a large number of professionals. Away back in 1901 the ratio of males working in the different professions in the Morayshire capital was at 6 per cent even higher than Edinburgh's. When, however, the

The Moray Floods of 1915
Ploughing its Way out of B.R. Station, Elgin

A dramatic scene at the former Highland Railway station in 1915.

Town Council claimed city-status for their burgh, their claim, asserted on the basis that Elgin was a former cathedral town, received no official sanction. Indeed when, at the time of Queen Victoria's Jubilee, the Lord Provosts of the acknowledged cities received commemorative gold medals, Elgin, like the other Scottish burghs, received just a silver one. It is said that Elgin Town Council, feeling pit oot by this affront, returned the silver medal but none-the-less failed to receive a gold one.

At least Elgin is one of the few towns in the three counties that still possesses a passenger railway station (the others are Keith, Forres and Nairn). Most of the rest went in the 1960s when British Rail slashed services and lines. For this writer, although I was away from the area by then, the closure of the Coast Line was greatly regretted. Some of my earliest memories from childhood days in Buckie are of being lifted up so that I could see over the railway fence and watch the trains go by.

CHAPTER 10

'Brightons of the North'

'I shall leave the stinking hot streets soon and get to the sea bath, which I long to be plunged in . . . it is so hot here, I wish to be in the sea at Macduff!'

The Earl of Fife, whose heartfelt plea was written in London in May 1784, was certainly an enthusiastic sea-bather, but so too were many of his contemporaries. The Brodies of Brodie — male and female alike — were also keen dookers. They holidayed at Lossiemouth, where they owned a house, for the 'restorative' benefits of sea-bathing.

The medicinal overtones in the word 'restorative' give a clue as to the origins of this particular fashion. Sea-bathing, or 'the salt water cure' as it had come to be called, was an extension of a much older health fad — namely, drinking from, or bathing in, mineral springs or wells. In contrast to the medieval holy wells, the mineral content of the so-called 'medicinal' wells had been analysed by 'scientific' experts. Among the most popular mineral waters were those with a saline (i.e. salt) content, and it was but a short step to the realisation that the sea was full of salt and that sea-water was an equally effective purgative. Accordingly, some 18th century medical practitioners began to send their upper-class patients to resorts like Nairn where in 1793 there was, as we have already seen, a bathing machine on the beach 'for the accommodation of persons who require the benefit of the salt bath.' Sea air was also then recommended for its 'restorative' qualities, particularly for pulmonary complaints. We find, for instance, Mrs Grant of Laggan — this was in June 1791 — bringing her daughter 'who had a threatening illness' down from Badenoch to her father's residence at Fort George 'for sea air'.

Sea-bathing was then so popular that the healthy no less than the sick made annual pilgrimages to the coast. Nairn was visited every summer by 'folk from the hills' — humble country-dwellers, who lodged in the fisher toun. They were probably more appreciative than Elizabeth Grant of Rothiemurchus who described 'this odious fisher place' to be comfortless and dreary. It was August when they came — 'the period of Lammas-tide when the waters of the ocean were supposed to possess a peculiar medicinal efficacy.' That was the time of the year, too, when crowds of poor people from the Lancashire milltowns walked to a seaside village called Blackpool. They likewise believed that in the months of August and September there was 'physic in the sea — physic of a most comprehensive description, combining all the virtues of all the drugs in the doctor's shop, and of course a cure for all varieties of disease.'

Buckie and Portsoy had likewise become places of resort, although on a smaller scale perhaps than Blackpool. Their attractions included, as well as sea bathing, mineral springs which were valued for their chalybeate (i.e. iron-impregnated) water. As its name implies, the Red Well of Boyndie was also a chalybeate spring. This well, which is situated between Whitehills and Banff, enjoyed a considerable reputation. The parish minister of Banff, writing in 1797, expressed some reservations, however. Since the Red Well of Boyndie was regarded by the country people as 'a Panacea' for all sorts of diseases, it was being misused by them. Unlike the gentry and professional classes, who had both the time and the resources for a lengthy stay, the countryfolk, unaccustomed to the leisurely forms of treatment that were the rule in genteel watering-places, were 'often known to swallow three gallons a-day ... besides a reasonable potion of sea-water.' But the country folk seemingly took no heed of such warnings. Indeed we are told by a later writer that the Red Well of Boyndie, together with a similar well at Tarlair near Macduff, was so highly valued 'that the farm servants, at the distance of from 30 to 40 miles, make it a part of the agreement with their masters that they shall be allowed two weeks in the month of July or August to attend these wells.'

Like the Boyndie well, the Tarlair spring was conveniently close to the sea. Discovered apparently in 1770, Tarlair water was recommended for kidney and bladder complaints. The Earl of Fife built an approach road and wellhouse, which, incidentally, was demolished in 1972 after a wartime explosion blocked the spring. In *Johnny Gibb of Gushetneuk*, that delightful novel about Aberdeenshire farming folk, William Alexander vividly describes the Wells of Tarlair, as they were in the 1830s. Countryfolk, the novelist wrote, 'believed in the Wells, old and young of them. Elderly people, male and female, went to Macduff to benefit by the bracing effects of sea-bathing, combined with a course more or less rigorous of sea water taken internally, followed up by the mineral water of Tarlair; sturdy bairns were taken thither in troops for the cure of "scabbit faces" and "sic like"; youths and maidens, whose complaints often seemed not of a deadly nature, went to the Wells as they could contrive to get . . .'

Some places with mineral springs became fashionable watering-places or spas, including for a time Peterhead and Pannanich Wells near Ballater. Since successful spas brought prestige and financial rewards, hopeful entrepreneurs tried to claim that their local springs were as good or even better than the chalybeate waters at Pannanich springs and the equally famous 'Wine Well' at Peterhead. In the parish of Kirkmichael there was a spring, which was reckoned to be superior to the Deeside wells. According to the Rev John Grant, this well was 'much frequented by people troubled with the stone, or labouring under stomachic complaints'.

Although medical fashions changed, the vogue for seaside holidays continued unabated. Burghead and Findhorn, for instance, were favoured by 'respectable' families from Elgin and Forres. Pleasant walks and comfortable lodging-houses were among their attractions. Burghead according to 'The Scottish Tourist' (1834 edition), was accessible by sea with 'steam yachts', sailing during the summer months on a weekly run between Edinburgh and Inverness, calling at that port (and also Banff). During the early years of the 19th century Elgin businessmen also began to erect holiday villas at Stotfield and the new planned village of Branderburgh.

The real boom in tourist growth came with the development of the railway system, starting with the Morayshire Railway's Elgin to Lossiemouth line in 1852. Then in 1855 the Highland Railway linked Nairn to Inverness. The subsequent development of trunk railway services was of inestimable benefit to Nairn and other Moray coast resorts. By the 1880s more than half of the visitors to Nairn came from London and

Edwardian Nairn on a windy (i.e. bracing) day. Notice the bathing-machines.

the south of England. Nairn had been put on the map of fashionable Victorian health resorts by Dr John Grigor, an eminent and well-connected physician, who was backed by an 'improving' town council. Thanks in large part to Dr Grigor's connections, fashionable London physicians knew about Nairn's dry, bracing climate and so readily sent their wealthier patients north to recuperate. For fog-afflicted Londoners the quality of the air, that part of the Moray Firth coast being virtually free of fog and mist, was another recommendation. (This was an important factor, too, for the Air Ministry when in the late 1930s it established flying training bases at Lossiemouth and Kinloss). The kind of climate that suited tourists also attracted permanent residents. Quite a few retired military personnel and 'ex-colonials' settled in Nairn and also, it should be said, in nearby towns like Forres. In time, Nairn was also promoted as a winter resort. The self-styled 'Brighton of the North' was reckoned to be ideal for 'convalescents and overwrought brain workers, and as a place of "after-cure" following spa treatment.' Prospective convalescents had, it is to be hoped, not read 'The Ordnance Gazetteer of Scotland' which, after stating that the Northern Counties Convalescent Home was located at Nairn,

The large and handsome railway station at Nairn reflects its status as the erstwhile 'Brighton of the North'. (Photograph: the author)

continued in somewhat pessimistic vein by informing readers that there was also a cemetery east of the town.

Nairn, as with Lossiemouth and some other Moray coast towns and villages, had good bathing beaches. At the more fashionable resorts the facilities for bathing included a number of bathing machines. For less hardy dookers, indoor salt-water baths were seen as essential amenities. In the early nineteenth century a joint-stock company had built a suite of baths at Banff. Baths were also erected at Nairn, Burghead and rather later at Lossiemouth. The first bath house at Nairn was erected on the links in 1821. In 1873 Nairn took a major step forward with the construction of an imposing indoor swimming pool. Water for the baths, which were superlatively good for that era, was pumped from the sea. A suite of private baths, where patrons could be given seaweed, pine, peat and other forms of bath, was added later. Altered and modernised over the years, these historic baths were replaced by a new pond in 1983. The Royal Marine Hotel had its own baths where spa-type treatments were also available.

Gowf was another leisure-pursuit that helped attract visitors. Playing at 'the golff' has a long history in the north-east. In January 1596 Walter Hay, an Elgin goldsmith was 'accusit of playing at the boulis and golff upoun Sondaye in the tyme of the sermon'. Forty-five years later some of the citizens of Cullen likewise incurred the wrath of the session for joukin the kirk and for spending their Sunday afternoons 'playing at ye golff'. Their penalty, a fine and public censure, was at least more lenient than the death penalty imposed at Banff four years previously on a boy who had broken into a shop and stolen, among other objects, 'sume golff balls'. Lord Brodie was a golfer, but, typically for that puritanical laird, his conscience troubled him. He hoped that the attractions of the game would not prove to be a snare to him. When the featherie, which was very expensive to make, became the standard ball, the poorer sections of society were priced out of the game, until the 1840s when the rubber-like guttie came into use. At Nairn, while the fishermen played bools, with heavy iron balls, on the links, 18th century references would indicate that it was the gentlemen of the town who played the 'golff'. The loss of common land, as at Elgin in the 1760s, was another inhibiting factor.

It was not till the last quarter of the century that golf really took off. Gowf was played at different places along the coast — on links at, for example, Banff, Cullen, Strathlene (Buckie), Lossie and Nairn. Since links were utilised for a variety of purposes, the golfers didn't have things all their own way. Fishermens' nets laid out to dry were some of the hazards gowfers faced at Banff and Cullen. At Cullen too the 17th fairway also served as the football pitch — a circumstance which led to a certain conflict of interest. Eventually the game became better organised with golfing societies or clubs formed and courses formally delimited. When the 'upper crust' in England as well as Scotland began to take up the game, more clubs were formed and new courses laid out. The Nairn Club was formed in 1887 and the Moray, which plays at Lossiemouth links, two years later. Ladies' clubs were also formed and short courses constructed for their benefit and possibly, also, to keep them away from the male domain. At Nairn working-class gowfers were also segregated. In 1899 a separate course (9 holes originally) was laid out on land gifted by Sir Alexander

Dunbar. The fact that this links, Nairn Dunbar, was designed for 'the artisan class' shows quite clearly that Nairn was a socially stratified community.

The economic benefits of golf-course and clubhouse investment were seen most markedly at Nairn and Lossiemouth. In both towns villas to let to tourists were built next to the links. The Lossie course was so successful that within a few years a new prestigious hotel, the Stotfield, was built. Lossiemouth made such rapid progress that soon other hotels were erected and the Stotfield itself had to be greatly enlarged. To enhance Lossie's new-found status as a fashionable watering-place, the kirk session decided that a new kirk was required that would be more 'in keeping with the new character of the locality as a rising summer resort.' During the fishing depression of the interwar years, well-to-do summer residents gave the new St Gerardine's the kind of financial support that was once the function of the heritors. As in other towns, the Victorian enthusiasm for organised sports saw provision for tennis courts and bowling greens, which like golf courses were now deemed to be essential amenities. The ambitious resort also of course published an assortment of guide-books which highlighted such facilities and stressed too its climatic pre-eminence. The Lossie rainfall, states a 1920s guide, 'compares favourably with that of Hastings, Harrogate, Strathpeffer, or Nairn.' For a guide-book it is unusually honest in drawing attention to the fact that 'winds may be somewhat prevalent'. But then the writer speedily adds that 'laden as they are with health-giving ozone, they act as a "filip" to the tired town worker in need of an invigorating climate.' Obviously not in the business of lavishing praise on rival resorts, the editor says that the popular resort of Nairn has splendid golfing and bathing facilities but that, apart from these, 'there is little to attract the attention.'

Nairn, however, had been managing very well, its population rising by some 70 per cent between 1841 and 1911 — i.e. from 2,672 to 4,661. (The population, it should be said, declined in the interwar period as a result of the fishing industry slump.) There was so much new construction that little of the old Nairn survived. One project, however, came to naught — namely, a proposal to construct a promenade pier. If it had been built, Nairn would have have been the only resort in Scotland, apart from Portobello, to have had such a pier. The first hotel like much else in the new Nairn was Dr Grigor-inspired. This was the homely-named Marine Hotel and Family Boarding-House, which built as it was in 1860 pre-dated the golfing boom. An early brochure, while lauding the facilities for sea-bathing, makes absolutely no reference to the game of golf. The hotel's subsequent change of name to the Royal Marine, and consequent rise in social cachet, followed a brief visit by one of Queen Victoria's daughters and her husband, the dreary Prince Christian, who came from the ponderously-named duchy of Schleswig-Holstein-Sonderburg-Augustenburg.

At Forres, already locally regarded as the 'Montpellier of Scotland', a revival of interest in water therapy saw the establishment in 1864 of a hotel specialising in different forms of water-cure or hydrotherapy. At this hotel — the Cluny Hill Hydropathic Establishment — health-conscious Victorians could take a variety of baths, ranging from Turkish to cold-water sprays. Enjoying a sheltered location, it became popular with valetudinarians seeking a sheltered winter resort. In time, the vogue for the water-cure and hydros passed. The Cluny Hill Hydro became the Cluny Hill Hotel. With golf course and other sports facilities, it catered for some years for a more general holiday market. This former hydro is now the Cluny Hill College and is owned by the Findhorn Foundation 'an international spiritual community' founded in 1962 at, as its name obviously suggests, the nearby village of Findhorn.

Further east the Banffshire fishing ports saw some tourist-related developments. In the early 1900s, some of the leading citizens of Cullen, aware no doubt of the wealth-producing developments at Nairn and Lossiemouth, pushed for the development of facilities such as a bowling green and tennis courts. Since it was apparent that Cullen was in decline as a fishing port, an influx of visitors would, they realised, bring valuable economic returns. Cullen Golf Club certainly advertised both its attractions and its accessibility — just 6½ hours train journey from Glasgow and 14 from London. No alcohol available at the clubhouse, however! Instead players could purchase aerated waters at 2d per bottle. Since it too had an interest in the economic fortunes of the towns and villages served by its Coast Line, the Great North of Scotland Railway

Tarlair swimming pool at Macduff was a popular destination with picnic parties: a 1930s view.

promoted the resorts of this area as the Moray Firth Riviera. There were too on offer, as early as 1901, golfing holiday promotions. Members of the local golf clubs could obtain cheap return railway tickets which would allow them to visit other courses in the area. It was too in the interests of the GNOSR and its successor the LNER to promote the attractions of Spey Bay Golf Club course. This new course was completed in 1907 with the adjacent hotel following shortly after.

In the 1930s there was a surge of interest in outdoor sports and activities, which led to the construction of a number of outdoor swimming pools. Two such ponds were constructed at Strathlene and Tarlair by the municipal authorities of Buckie and Macduff respectively. In their time they were considerable assets both as local facilities and as tourist attractions. This writer has fond memories of the now sadly derelict Strathlene pool. When just a wee loon, I taught myself to swim there, and later in the early 1950s when a student at Aberdeen University I was pool custodian at Strathlene for two successive summers, although having, it must be confessed, none of the qualifications which nowadays would be mandatory. Contrary to today's orthodoxies, Buckie Town Council, like many other councils, owned and operated a wide range of amenities. These included, in addition to the swimming pool, the adjacent Strathlene Hotel and Restaurant, two golf-courses, putting-greens, tennis-courts and caravan-site. In those days that was, of course, considered to be 'enlightened policy'.

But holiday patterns have changed since the days when 'summer residents' came year after year to the same resort and when a special sleeping car transported privileged southerners from London's King's Cross station to Lossiemouth. Distance did lead to enchantment as seaside towns like Lossie and Nairn offered seclusion. For the well-to-do a major attraction was the absence of large industrial towns. That meant that, unlike say the south coast resorts, there were no day-tripping hordes and no risk, therefore, of close encounters of an unwelcome kind. For graphic autobiographical accounts of childhood holidays at Nairn in those halcyon days of the interwar years, see Ludovic Kennedy's 'On My Way to the Club' and David Thomson's 'Nairn: In Darkness and Light'. Most holiday-makers, though, came from nearer at hand and from very different backgrounds. Right along the coast the busiest period of the year was the time of the Glasgow Fair. The visitors from the industrial belt, though, showed that, by avoiding the large, popular resorts and opting instead for the peace and quiet of wee places like Portsoy and Hopeman, they were in their own way just as selective and discerning as the golf club sets of Nairn and Lossie.

Today there are fewer long-stay visitors and, for those who do come, caravans are more popular than the villas and boarding-houses of yesteryear. There are, on the other hand, many more touring holiday-makers, very many of them from abroad. With popular centres at Findhorn and at the revamped Nairn harbour, yachting now has many devotees and the gowf-courses still attract those who worship that devilish wee white ball. Valetudinarian 'early-morning-dip' sea-dookers are, one suspects, less numerous than in Dr Grigor's day. Dookers still take the plunge but, not surprisingly perhaps, they prefer the hedonistic warmth of the area's many heated indoor ponds. It was perhaps a sign of the times when some years ago the statue of Dr John Grigor was flitted from Nairn's High Street to the grounds

Nairn Museum fronted by the bronze statue of Dr John Grigor. (Photograph: the author)

of Viewfield House. But then this Georgian mansion, which serves as the Nairn Museum and Literary Institute, is, or should be, a mecca for today's new-model 'cultural tourist'.

CHAPTER 11

Highland Sports and Whisky Trails

The rivers, straths and mountains of upland Banff, Moray, and Nairn also proved attractive to tourists. The poor roads and means of travel that are described in the chapter on transport constricted development, however. Even so a few wealthy sportsmen were lured north by the abundance of fish and game. A pioneer in this respect was the exceedingly wealthy Colonel Thornton who came to Strathspey to fish and shoot in the 1780s. This eccentric Yorkshireman, transported vast quantities of baggage, much of it, along with some servants, being shipped by sea from Hull to Findhorn. The natives, of course, had long been accustomed to fish the rivers and shoot wild game. On the carved stones of the ancient Picts hunting scenes were one of the favourite themes. In the Middle Ages, too, kings and noblemen enjoyed hunting stags, wild boar and other game in the forests of their north-eastern estates. It was once custom to hold tinchels or great hunts when large crowds of retainers were employed to drive deer and other game over the hills towards a particular glen or defile. When the hapless beasts arrived having been driven towards and into the trap by the beaters, the nobility and gentry were enabled to slaughter great quantities of game. A tinchel involved such large numbers that, when the Earl of Mar started the first Jacobite Rising, he used the pretext of a deer-hunt to explain why he had brought so many armed men to Braemar in September 1715.

After the failure of the Rising the Mar estate was forfeited and purchased by Lord Braco. His heir, James 2nd Earl of Fife, was a fanatical and extremely active deer-stalker. His correspondence, mainly letters he wrote to William Rose, his factor at Banff, (published in 1925 under the title of 'Lord Fife and his Factor') is a fascinating source of evidence for this and other aspects of 18th century life and society. When hunting from his base at old Mar Lodge, he traversed great tracts of very rough and difficult ground. Writing in August 1779, Lord

Good roads and signposted tourist trails make things easier for today's visitors. Off the beaten track, though, there are still many wild places accessible only to intrepid footsloggers. (Photograph: the author)

Fife described a typical day's sport when he was out on the hills from three in the morning till past eleven at night. 'My great fatigue,' he testified, 'was crowned with pleasure, glory and success, and do figure me at one o'clock in the heat of the day on the Cairngorum hill stripping off my shirt, to dray [dry] in the sun . . .' Although suffering all sorts of mishaps, the Earl really revelled in feats of endurance such as pursuing a wounded deer to the 'very farthest end of Glenguisachan, pitch dark, having lost everybody' and having had nothing to eat since six in the morning. He had to stumble back in the dark, tumbling from one hole to another and endeavouring, as he wrote, to 'smell my way to Mar Lodge in this terrible state'. Mar Lodge estate, it may be interposed, is currently attracting a lot of attention since conservation groups are attempting (this is early 1992) to raise sufficient funds to purchase this 77,000 acre estate for the nation.

To the north of the Cairngorms, the forests of Glenfiddich and Blackwater were, according to the Old Statistical Account, 'stored with red deer and roes; the hills all around with

innumerable flocks of muir-fowl.' Like his rival the Earl of
Fife, the Duke of Gordon was keen on field-sports including
falconry. In the 1790s he possessed a romantically situated
shooting lodge on the banks of the River Fiddich and another
further up on the Blackwater. While for such enthusiastic
sportsmen a herd of red deer was a magnificent sight, the
smallholders living close to the moors were less appreciative.
For the farmers red deer that came down on to low ground
were an unmitigated nuisance, since they consumed their crops
and destroyed young trees. In the late 18th century indeed the
Earl of Moray kept hounds to protect his plantations from the
depredations of deer.

Although the proprietors generally disapproved of poachers,
there were, nevertheless, keen shooters and fishermen in all
social groups. The landlords' disapprobation was intensified
as they began to appreciate that there were financial rewards
to be realised from letting their deer forests. As with the
whisky smugglers — of whom more anon — many tales are
told about the legendary 'free foresters' (or, in the landlords'
terms, poachers) and their exploits and feats of endurance.
There were hard men among the gamekeepers too — like
Robert Willox, the Duke of Gordon's forester in Glen Avon.
Pursuing two poachers in November 1762, Willox pointed his
gun at them and threatened, with a vivid turn of phrase, to
'make Sun and Moon shine through .. their bodies if they
did not stand.' Alexander Davidson (1792–1843) was one
of the most redoubtable of the free foresters. This hardy
Highlander roamed freely from the Dee to the Spey and even
further beyond. Although some landowners cast a blind eye on
his activities. Sir George Macpherson Grant of Ballindalloch
was one of the exceptions. When the Laird of Ballindalloch
apprehended him for shooting on the Braes of Avon, Sandy
Davidson got his revenge by going back again and again to
the laird's lands. The muirs of Ballindalloch, he averred, paid
handsomely for the £5 fine imposed on him. The stories about
Davidson are included in W. McCombie Smith's 'The Romance
of Poaching in the Highlands' which was first published in
1904. Davidson became a professional poacher after failing as
a timber merchant, for which failure the author blamed the
Earl of Fife of the time. McCombie Smith, incidentally, was

no admirer of the Duff/Fife dynasty, describing Lord Braco
as a 'money-lending usurer'. Tom Johnston, author of the
violently polemical 'Our Noble Families', was also critical. This
future Secretary of State assailed the Duffs for their 'thieving
propensities'.

Sport was only one of the reasons why more visitors came to
the north-east. Writers, like James 'Ossian' Macpherson and Sir
Walter Scott, helped to create an image of Scotland as a land
of romance and picturesque beauty. As the author of 'A Guide
to the Highlands of Speyside' remarked in 1852 — 'When Scott
adopted the Highlands as a subject of romantic song and story
then began a new era of comfort in every spot which his magic
touched.' Four years earlier Queen Victoria and Prince Albert
had holidayed on Deeside for the first time. Their subsequent
purchase of Balmoral as a sporting estate was a further boost
to the holiday trade. Other wealthy southerners followed their
example by buying or taking estates on let for deer-stalking,
grouse-shooting and fishing. Charles St John was one of the
new breed of sporting incomers. After sampling different
parts of the Highlands, he settled in Moray where he spent
his days shooting and fishing and also studying wild life. His
experiences and observations as a naturalist are detailed in his
'Natural History and Sport in Moray'. First published in 1846
this work is retitled, in later editions, 'Wild Sports and Natural
History of the Highlands'. As with other sportsmen of his day,
he shot pretty well anything and everything. Birds of prey like
the osprey, peregrine falcon, and eagle were blasted out of the
air. Occasionally, though, he did have regrets as when, after
shooting an eagle, he wrote — 'I looked with great regret at the
body of the noble bird and wished that I had not killed him.'

While salmon fishing has a long history, it was pursued, at
Speymouth and at other river estuaries and along the coast, on
an industrial basis rather than as a sport. Since the 13th century
at least salmon had been a major export. The right to the
fishings on the Spey belonged to Urquhart Priory. In the late
18th century, the Earls of Fife and the Dukes of Gordon, for
instance, drew handsome revenues from leasing salmon fishing
rights on the Deveron and Spey respectively. In the 1790s, and
for long thereafter, so many fish were being netted on the rivers
and by stake-nets along the coast that complaints were made

The old-style salmon fishers used coracles like this one in Elgin Museum. (Photograph: the author)

that too few fish were finding their way up stream. At that time, it may be noted, quite a few proprietors, including Lord Fife, had no interest in angling. For the landed proprietors, though, netting continued to be an exceedingly profitable business. With over 130 men employed in the 1790s, netting was a major source of employment at Speymouth and in the neighbouring parish of Bellie. In the 1840s there were 12 crews each with 7 or 8 men. So many fish were caught in the season, which at that time lasted from the 1st of February until mid-September, that from 8 to 12 smacks, sailing on a shuttle basis, were needed to carry salmon to the London market. Since most of the fish was transported in ice, a large store house for ice was built in 1830 at Tugnet on the eastern shore. It was almost certainly a replacement for an older building. Ice houses on a smaller scale were built elsewhere on the coast including Findhorn and Portsoy.

Netting was not confined to the river mouths and the coast. Up river on the Findhorn, the Earl of Moray had a remunerative fishery at Sluie where 4 men were employed to fish, using boat and nets, in certain deep pools. In 1842, it was reported, the average annual catch was 700 salmon. The company, which leased the netting rights, also employed a man to catch fish at a particular waterfall. The fisher used a clip, a long-handled gaff with several 'crooked prongs'. Seating himself on a rock below the fall, he held the clip about 6 inches under the water and waited for a salmon to be driven to the water's edge by the force of the fall. Then, as we are told, the fisherman 'by a sudden jerk with his instrument seldom fails to place it on the rock beside him.' Incidentally, where these salmon fishers once lived and worked there is now an attractive waymarked path skirting the spectacular Sluie Gorge. Another tenant whose lands ran alongside the Linn of Avon employed a simpler, and labour-saving, method of taking salmon. He just strung a capacious bag-net from a beam across the river at the Linn of Avon. Salmon that failed to loup the falls just fell into the bag.

In earlier days, before the full development of river-mouth trapping and netting, very many more fish had been caught. Salmon were so abundant that it was common, we are told, for 'servants entering in an engagement with any farmer resident on the banks of the Findhorn to stipulate that they should not be fed upon salmon beyond a stated number of days in the week.' The common people, too, were accustomed to take fish as they needed, catching trout and salmon by a variety of methods. They fished with nets, clips, rods and fish-spears. The fish-spear, or leister, was often used at night when the river was 'blazed' by torch-light. In 1850, the royal household at Balmoral were spectators when the locals were leistering and netting salmon on the Dee. Albert even had a go at what Victoria saw — this was in daytime — as an 'exciting and picturesque' spectacle.

With 'fishing gentlemen' in ever increasing numbers seeking out our northern lochs and rivers, the proprietors, just as they were doing with the grouse-muirs and deer-forests, began to treat their freshwater fisheries as commercial assets. When salmon lets became profitable, traditional methods of catching like burning or blazing the river were prohibited. Although allowed to fish the lesser burns, the sma folk were shut out from the best river beats. These well-to-do visitors demanded a

The Pole Inn near Tomintoul was once a drovers' inn. The name comes from the Gaelic 'poll' meaning a pool, a hole or a muddy field. (Photograph: the author)

better standard of inn, as the Rev Thomas Grierson observed in 1848. While travelling in the north-east, he noted that the inns seemed to be 'extremely well kept and comfortable, which is mainly owing to the district being much frequented by wealthy sportsmen during the shooting and fishing seasons . . .'

As salmon fishing became more prestigious and thus even more lucrative, the riparian owners now sought to reduce the numbers caught by the netsmen. In 1907 the netting rights on the Deveron were purchased from the Duke of Fife. Around that time, too, the Duke of Richmond and Gordon removed the nets from a 7 mile stretch of the Spey. On the River Nairn, already a good trouting river, a weir was demolished to give salmon a better run. In recent years more nets have been removed. In the 1980s the Atlantic Salmon Conservation Trust started to buy up and close a number of nettings which, it claimed, were creaming off the best fish and thus depriving anglers of their sport and, of course, of the rents that proprietors derived from letting angling rights. For this and other reasons there has been a very considerable drop in the number of salmon taken by commercial netsmen. The techniques and equipment utilised on the Spey and elsewhere can be viewed at the excellent exhibition centre in the former ice house at Tugnet at Spey Bay.

The rise in popularity of angling and other 'wild sports' helped bring visitors to Speyside villages like Fochabers, Craigellachie, and Aberlour. Early August was a particularly busy time as the grouse shooting season started on the 12th of August ('The Glorious Twelfth'). Special trains sped northward, carrying the rich and the famous, their carriages and servants to Strathspey and other Highland destinations. As the sporting interests of the leisured classes widened, communities like Aberlour provided the recreational facilities that their visitors now required. Edwardian Aberlour had a 9 hole golf course, tennis courts and two bowling greens.

Grantown-on-Spey was another sportsman's mecca which gained from the development in Victorian times of 'a recreation economy'. A subsequently well publicised visit by Queen Victoria in 1860 and the arrival of the railway three years later boosted Grantown's popularity. Strathspey's dry bracing climate was an additional asset. As with other villages in the area, Grantown's climatic virtues were lauded by eminent medical practitioners. The extensive pine woods with their sheltered walks were widely appreciated. According to 'Health Resorts of the British Isles' (1912), those 'requiring rest and quiet on account of nervous overstrain and debility are greatly benefited by the stillness of the woods and the privileges extended to visitors who can roam about the country without hindrance.' In an age when game conscious Highland landlords tried to keep walkers and climbers out of their estates, this kind of privilege was a great advantage. With the Highland and Great North Railways bringing increasing numbers of tourists, local businessmen seized their opportunities. New villas and hotels were erected, with tradesmen and specialist retailers making and hiring out furniture for holiday homes. Local organisations provided facilities for golf, bowls and tennis. In 1914 an Angling Improvement Association was established. Equally important were such amenities as a public hall for concerts and a variety of kirks (with Episcopalian services in the summer for southern

Advertisement postcard for a 'Boarding Residence' at Grantown which, considerably extended, is now a hotel. The card was posted in July 1914: the sender had been at Grantown for nearly 4 weeks, greatly enjoying the lovely walks and the 'fine pure air'.

visitors). Visitors too were reassured to know that Grantown possessed a gravitational water supply (1881) and that there were resident doctors.

Grantown, though, like other resorts had to adapt to change. By the 1930s the pattern of holidays had altered. With domestic servants hard to come by, the middle classes were no longer renting houses for long periods. Some villas were, accordingly, converted into boarding-houses and hotels. Although many people were opting for touring holidays by car or bus, Grantown did succeed in attracting a fair number of long-stay visitors, thanks to improvements that were wrought on, for example, the golf course and tennis courts. The Grantown Open Tennis Tournament became a notable event and attracted many competitors. But with many of the 'toffs' going elsewhere, new markets had to be found. When in the 1930s hiking and other outdoor activities became more popular, some farmers provided camp-sites. They realised that catering for open-air enthusiasts could be a useful source of income. In the mid-20th century, visitors, particularly the young, were eager to try other forms of sport. Pony trekking and winter sport packages were introduced, the latter activity having the major advantage of filling hotel beds in the dead season. Although attempts to promote the area for curling, skating and other winter sports went back a long way, it was only in the 1950s that serious efforts were made to promote skiing holidays. With the support of the Scottish Council for Physical Recreation, four Grantown hotels organised inclusive skiing holidays. Skiing, though, did not really take off until 1960–1 when a chair lift and access road were built on the 1,245 metre high Cairngorm mountain. The main benefit from the winter sports boom, however, went to villages like Aviemore which are closer to the Cairngorm skiing facilities. Big business chose Aviemore rather than Grantown as a centre for large-scale development. Grantown hoteliers resented what they saw as a takeover, with big business reaping 'a crop that had been planted by local sweat and money.' From the aesthetic point of view, if no other, this concentration on the 'Aviemore-Cairngorm corridor' was perhaps fortunate for Grantown. Regrettably, though, influential area tourist organisations downgraded their own heritage and culture by casting aside historic names like Badenoch and Strathspey and adopting for promotional purposes the blandly anglicised Spey Valley. Some opponents have, however, covered over the words Spey Valley on some tourist route signs by rivetting on metal plates bearing the linguistically correct name of Strathspey.

Place-names like Strathspey are, like many others even in the lowland areas, derived from Gaelic. (A strath means a wide valley). Gaelic was once widely spoken in the north-east. Even as late as the 1840s there were around 200 Gaelic speakers in the parish of Forres. Since they were in the main elderly people, the language was then obviously in decline. Census returns chart the downturn. By 1931 there were only 943 Gaelic speakers in the counties of Moray and Nairn. Twenty years later the number had dwindled to 408. The situation in Banffshire was even worse. Once, in the upper part of the county, kirk services had been conducted in Gaelic, but in the former linguistic stronghold of Tomintoul the last Gaelic service was held in 1872. By 1951 the language was considered dead in the county of Banff.

If tourism was one growth area, the whisky industry was another. The 19th century boom in whisky sales boosted the rural economy. Speyside villages and many other north-east communities benefited from the newfound popularity of whisky. While Highlanders had made uisge beatha or 'the Water of Life' for their own use or for local distribution, it did not become widely popular, however, until the 18th century. Because restrictive legislation and increased excise duties encouraged illegal production, distilling changed from being a sideline to a mainstream activity. For farmers and smallholders, particularly those on the economic margins of society, ownership of a small still could be highly profitable, especially since the capital outlay was inconsiderable. The Cabrach in the Highlands of Banffshire and Aberdeenshire was the kind of area where illicit distilling was one of the staple occupations. A knowledgeable observer described the situation as he saw it in 1823. 'The people there are remarkably poor, it is a very cold district; the grain does not ripen there very well, and the breeding of black cattle, and the universal smuggling, forms the whole trade and occupation of the people.' Tomintoul was another centre of the trade. The villagers being left by the proprietor, the Duke of Gordon, 'to pursue the occupation most agreeable to them', elected, according to the late 18th century parish minister, to make and sell whisky. When not so engaged, the women, this clergyman waspishly added, 'spin yarn, kiss their inamoratos, or dance to the discordant strain of an old fiddle.' At that time too the demand, especially from the Scottish lowlands, for good quality highland malt whisky had increased. The increase in spirit drinking was one which 18th-century clergymen deplored, but then, as the minister at Mortlach complained, it was the same with tea — 'The drinking of whisky instead of good ale is a miserable change, and so likewise is the very general use of tea. These put together have been exceedingly hurtful to both health and morals.'

Nevertheless, consumers who sought a quality dram were willing to pay a higher price for highland malt as opposed to lowland grain whisky. 'Glenlivet' especially fetched a good price since that was the whisky favoured by the 'higher orders of people', including seemingly King George IV. Not surprisingly, there were, it was reckoned in 1822, 200 sma stills operating in Glenlivet. The small stills of Glenlivet indeed became so profitable that the inhabitants abandoned crofting and did nothing else. It was not just the men who were involved. The females, as one minister disapprovingly reported, spent a lot of time in the pot-still bothy 'by night as well as by day . . . a prey to the licentious and immoral.' Grain for the stills were procured from farmers from lowland Moray and Banff who, for their part, were only too pleased to have a ready market for their surplus stocks of barley. Copious supplies of peat were available to dry the grain. For law enforcers, though, upland areas like the Cabrach and the Braes of Glenlivet were difficult to patrol, the more especially since the illicit distillers and smugglers were quite prepared to resort to force to protect their interests. The fact that many landowners, including some magistrates, turned a blind eye to illegal distilling added to the revenue men's problems.

Once distilled the whisky was carried to lowland towns and others selling points by professional smugglers. The smugglers, who were heavily armed and travelled in convoy, stuck to remote hill tracks. One eyewitness wrote of them in approving terms: 'There was something attractive and romantic in the smuggler's calling. We have seen congregated associations of daring spirits, in bands of from ten to twenty men, with as many horses, with two ankers of whisky on the back of each horse, wending their way, singing in joyous chorus along the winding banks of the Avon; one man carrying a small barrel on his back . . . and all and sundry coming in contact with the band were invited to drink . . .' Others, though, saw it as a pernicious trade that led to lawlessness. As one clergyman wrote — 'night was turned into day, the farm and family neglected, and all credit and character perilled in this demoralizing manufacture and traffic.'

But from 1822 the government intensified action against the trade, increasing and extending the system of penalties and employing the military to back up the excisemen. Although, as elsewhere in the Highlands, many tales were told of successful skirmishes and of the tricks and stratagems employed to deceive the gaugers, nevertheless the illegal whisky trade was ultimately suppressed. In addition to coercive methods, the government also held out a carrot. Encouraged by the Duke of Gordon, the government passed the Excise Act of 1823 which reduced the duties and fees for legal distilleries. Entrepreneurs, including some lairds, started up distilleries. Even comparatively small-scale producers were able to enter the legal trade. In 1824, for instance, John Cumming, the tenant-farmer at Cardow at Knockando took out a licence for a small still that was operated as part of the farm. Not that John Cumming and his wife were new to the business. As they had been distilling illegally, they had developed the appropriate skills. But for long Cardow, with the distillery just part of the farm, remained a small-scale enterprise. George Smith of Upper Drumin was another illicit distiller who turned his coat. Paying his licence fee, he built a new distillery in 1824. As he resided in Glenlivet, an area that was jam-packed with illegal 'sma stills', George Smith soon found himself under threat. Sticking a pair of pistols in his belt and likewise arming a few 'stout fellows for servants', he passed the word around that he would fight for his distillery till the last shot. 'But,' as he testified, 'I often both at kirk and market had rough times of it among the Glen people, and if it had not been for the ... pistols, I don't think I should have been telling this story now.' Built in the first place at Drumin, this distillery which markets 'The Glenlivet' was transferred to its present site in 1858.

From the mid-19th century spirit merchants started blending lowland grain whisky with the single malts that were the special product of Speyside and other northern stills. The Highland single malts made from malted barley in pot-stills gave the grain whisky some taste, thus creating a palatable blend. These blended and branded whiskies were skilfully marketed and became increasingly popular. Slow growing planned villages like Rothes, Aberlour and Dufftown profited from the new distilleries that were built. Glen Grant in 1840 was the first in Rothes. Keith and Craigellachie, which was a Victorian creation, also gained from the growth of the whisky trade. Rothes now has four and Keith three distilleries. The trade and the developing communities of Speyside and of the other whisky producing areas benefited in their turn from the expansion of the railways.

A sales boom saw many new distilleries founded and others enlarged and modernised. In the 1880s whisky sales were given a fortuitous boost when phylloxera devastated the vineyards of the continental brandy and wine producers. A significant number of the north-east distilleries were built in the period of prosperity that followed. In the counties of Banff and Moray 19 new distilleries were constructed between 1894 and 1899.

William Grant, for example, who was manager at Mortlach Distillery, seized his opportunities at the right time, purchasing second-hand equipment from Cardow in 1886. Aided by his seven sons and two daughters, he started to construct the now renowned Glenfiddich Distillery. Since, as with all the best malts, good water is crucial, William Grant chose a site where he could use water from a spring that had been highly valued in the old whisky smuggling days. With the whisky boom continuing, William Grant expanded, buying the lands of Balvenie from the 1st Duke of Fife for his Balvenie Distillery. Apparently, though, Balvenie is troubled by a spirit of a different kind. It is said that a ghost walks in one of the malt barns. But Dufftown was an ideal location for other operators too. As the local saying goes — 'While Rome was built on seven hills, Dufftown stood on seven stills.'

The whisky boom, however, was not to last. The bubble burst just as the century neared its close. In the following decades the situation grew worse thanks to the harshly selective duties levied on whisky by the Westminster government. Grants, for one, tried to find new custom by advertising their Glenfiddich malt as suitable for medicinal and family use. It was, they claimed, 'manufactured under the Careful and Personal Supervision of a Fully Qualified Doctor'. When the government of the United States, taking a contrary view, introduced prohibition in 1920, exports slumped. With the onset of world depression a number of distilleries shut down. The end of America's 'noble experiment' in 1933 helped towards a revival in exports and the reopening of distilleries like Dallas Dhu which had ceased production. In the post-1945 period, since whisky exports earned valuable foreign currency, production was encouraged. Starting with Glen Keith (at Keith) in 1957 a number of new distilleries have been erected. Also some old ones have been reopened or enlarged. Cardow, for example, where a new distillery had been built at the time of the late 19th century boom, was modernised in the 1960s: twenty years later the name

Dufftown — tourist resort and whisky-distilling centre. It was founded by James Duff, 4th Earl of Fife, whose family is commemorated in the town's name. (Photograph: the author)

was changed to Cardhu. Since the 1960s there have been ups and downs, with sales dipping in the early 1970s and again at the beginning of the following decade. With the trade finding new world markets, business had picked up again by the late 1980s, allowing mothballed distilleries to be reopened. One of the significant developments in recent years

The old railway station at Blacksboat on the Speyside Way. As the name suggests, this was one of the historic ferry sites on the River Spey. (Photograph: the author)

has been the thrust to promote and sell single malt whiskies, many from the distilleries of Banff and Moray. Expansion has brought substantial investment in related areas — in, for example, maltings at Burghead, Buckie and elsewhere. Another significant form of employment is coopering. Since the industry requires wooden barrels to mature and store its whisky, the coopers at places like Keith and Craigellachie are kept busy. By 1989 the cooperage at Craigellachie was handling some 70,000 casks a year. Byproducts, too, are used more productively. For instance, the malting barley and yeast left after the starch and enzymes have been removed is now used to make animal feed instead of, as formerly, being dumped as waste.

Since 1969 when Glenfiddich set up the first distillery reception centre on Speyside, quite a few other whisky companies have followed suit, with both producers and tourist-promoting organisations promoting not just individual centres but also whisky trails. With their sophisticated and multi-lingual forms of presentation distillery visitor centres like Glenfiddich's

A modern distillery, Chivas Regal, in the Braes of Glenlivet. (Photograph: the author)

at Dufftown and Glen Grant's at Rothes have been turned into major tourist attractions. One which, because, it is no longer producing, opens more doors than usual is that Victorian 'time-capsule of the distiller's craft', Dallas Dhu near Forres, which is now under the care of Historic Scotland. As with other distillery visitor centres, a dram of the real cratur is provided free of charge.

For the many tourists who head for the rivers, hills and glens of the uplands of Banff, Moray and Nairn, there are many options. There is full scope for water-sport enthusiasts, bird-watchers, cyclists, hill-walkers, climbers, and skiers both downhill and cross-country. For walkers the Speyside Way, which includes a number of spurs, is an attractive and not too difficult long-distance footpath. Since the Way passes a number of distilleries, it affords opportunities for walkers to make diversions, if they are so inclined, and include in their itinerary some of the most famous of the Speyside malt distilleries. There are, however, other good footpaths in this Scottish malt whisky heartland. Some indeed follow the same paths that were used by the whisky smugglers of yesteryear.

CHAPTER 12

Defence of the Realms

*'There's naethin for fairmers like a gweed war; it aye keeps up the price
o corn.'*

While the outbreak of the First World War did benefit farmers
because of the unprecedented demand for foodstuffs, the
equally unprecedented casualty rates hardly compensated for
the short-lived wartime boom. As in the 19th-century wars, local
regiments like the Gordons, Seaforths and Camerons played a
notable part in all theatres of war. Even a cursory glance at the
area's war memorials reveals, though, the heavy price paid by
all the north-east communities. As well as contributing to the
military effort, many men from the coastal towns and villages
served with the navy and merchant navy. Nor was it just the
menfolk who went off to war. In 1914, with herring fishing
curtailed, large numbers of steam-drifters were requisitioned by
the Admiralty. From the White Sea to the Red Sea, the crews of
these adaptable vessels were employed on multifarious duties,
including dangerous anti-submarine work and mine-sweeping.
There were many casualties. From Macduff alone four drifters
were lost.

By the late 1930s the threat from Hitler's Germany necessitated preparations to protect the populace in the event of
air attack. Air raid precautions were instituted, with bomb
shelters built and gas masks issued. As part of the government's
rearmament programme new defence establishments were
created. In January 1938 the Air Ministry purchased nearly
1,000 acres of prime farm land for two new, permanent
aerodromes at Lossiemouth and Kinloss. These developments
gave welcome relief to the local unemployed. Once hostilities
commenced in September 1939 airfields were constructed at
other sites including Forres, Milltown, Boyndie near Banff and
Dallachy by Spey Bay. Planned as Flying Training Schools, they
were located in areas which, it was thought, would not be
open to enemy attack. When, however, the Germans occupied

The Munich crisis of 1938 saw the fleet mobilised. Here we see the local naval reservists marching to Buckie railway station. At the front (right) is the author's father acting as escort. On the same day — 29 September — Neville Chamberlain flew to meet Hitler at Munich, and subsequently returned with 'peace in our time'.

Norway, the situation changed. The north-east was now open to attack from aircraft flying across the North Sea from Norwegian bases. In October 1940 three enemy Heinkel bombers made a low level strike on the Lossiemouth air base. One of the German bombers was destroyed.

As in the previous war, the seamen of Moray, Banff, and Nairn, and their boats too served their country well. Many having already joined the Royal Naval Volunteer Reserve served from the outbreak of hostilities. On land, the north-east communities suffered a grievous blow when in June 1940 the 51st Highland Division was trapped at the French port of St Valery and many local servicemen were taken prisoner. German occupation of most of Europe meant an inflow of refugees. Later in the war allied troops, including many Poles, were stationed at Forres and other north-east towns and villages. After the fall of Denmark and Norway, sizeable numbers of Scandinavians, especially Norwegians, escaped across the North Sea. Quite a number stayed on in the area during the duration of the war, many fishing out of Buckie.

When in 1940 the Germans were preparing for an invasion of Britain, they sent over a number of spies to glean and send back vital information. Although some of their agents spoke little English, the hope was that they could pass themselves off as refugees. In the early hours of Monday 30th September 1940, a German seaplane, carrying three hastily trained agents, flew from Stavanger and touched down on the sea just west of Buckie. The agents, two men and a woman, had been instructed to make their way to the shore, using an inflatable rubber dinghy, then travel south by bicycle. Unfortunately for them the plane's crew were anxious to be up and away again and instead of going into the dinghy the bikes ended up in the sea. The hapless trio paddled towards dry land, eventually landing on a shingle beach between Buckie and Portgordon. Once ashore they split up. One of the males walked east towards Buckie where he hoped to find a train to take him to Aberdeen.

The others, who headed in the opposite direction, were an intriguingly odd pair. Although the male, Karl Theo Drucke, was well-educated, sophisticated and widely-travelled, he knew little English. His comely female companion, whose cover name was Vera Erikson, was a lady with a past, but she had lived in Britain and spoke the language well. Walking into nearby Portgordon, they reached the railway station around 7.30 a.m. Unluckily for them, their feet had got wet when they landed and this odd circumstance, allied to other discrepancies, put Porter John Geddes and Stationmaster John Donald on the alert. 'There's something queer about that pair,' Geddes observed. The stationmaster phoned Police Constable Grieve, the local bobby who, after examining their papers and observing some irregularities, asked them to accompany him to the village police station. There he phoned his superior officer, Inspector John Simpson at Buckie. When he reached Portgordon, Inspector Simpson — the author's father incidentally — first questioned the suspects and then searched Drucke. In one pocket he found a box with 19 rounds of revolver ammunition. On bursting open the suitcase that Drucke carried, the Inspector found a loaded Mauser pistol, a wireless transmitter, coding devices and other equipment for espionage. A general alert was sent out. When the beach was searched, a new pair of foreign-made rubber boots was discovered. Since, it was ascertained, a dog had barked furiously at a nearby house in the early morning, the police were convinced that they had identified the spot where the spies had landed. Since the boots did not fit the man who was already in their hands, the police knew that there was a third spy on the loose.

The hunt was now on for the 'third man' who, it was later learned, was Werner Heinrich Walti, a Swiss national. His movements were traced to Buckie railway station but he had already departed on the 9.58 a.m. train for Aberdeen. The Aberdeen police were informed and they ascertained that a man fitting the description that the Buckie police provided had joined a train to Edinburgh. The Edinburgh police now picked up the trail. Walti, they discovered, had deposited his case in the left luggage office at Waverley station. When the agent returned to collect it, plain-clothes detectives closed in on him. Walti tried to pull out his Mauser, but the Edinburgh men were too quick for him. All three spies were now in the bag. By this time, too, their dinghy, which they had tried unsuccessfully to destroy, had been discovered by the Buckie coastguard, rolled up but still floating a few hundred metres from the shore.

As to their fate, Walti and Drucke were tried at the Old Bailey and sentenced to death. They were hanged at Wandsworth on 6th August 1941. As for Vera the Beautiful Spy, as she was subsequently termed, she was definitely a stunner. According to my father's notes, made after her arrest, she was 5 foot tall and of slender build. Her hair was dark and her eyes dark grey. She spoke, or claimed to speak, English, French, Russian, German and Danish. Vera, however, escaped prosecution. A mystery woman with a shady past she had apparently been 'of some use to our authorities.' It has even been suggested that she had worked for the British before the war and that she was actually a double-agent. Whatever the truth may be, statements made by one writer on the subject that, when still with Drucke at Portgordon Police Station, Vera asked Inspector Simpson for a word in private is pure fabrication. Nor did she hand over to him any document with a special address, saying supposedly that 'Your authorities know all about this.' The author has, however, in his possession a souvenir of her short-lived visit

144 squadron at Dallachy near Spey Bay in Spring 1945. The twin-engined Beaufigher was a rocket-carrying strike aircraft.

to the Banffshire coast — namely a scrap of paper bearing her signature. The name she wrote down is, as I read it, Vera de Cottani Chalbur. This may be, of course, just one of the aliases she employed. After the war, she assumed a new identity and went to live, it was said, in the Isle of Wight.

While the Moray Firth coast towns were now, as we have seen, open to attack from German aircraft flying from Norway, the converse was also true. Although the RAF bases at Kinloss and Lossiemouth were utilised mainly for maintenance work and for training night bomber crews, they were also employed for strike operations against ships in Norwegian waters. The long-range bombers which attacked the 'Tirpitz', and which eventually sunk that formidable battleship, were refuelled at north-east airfields. With the training aircraft having to fly over the Cairngorms and other mountainous areas, a Mountain Rescue Unit was formed in 1944. There were indeed many tragic accidents on both land and sea, with almost 200 aircrew from Kinloss alone killed in training. Some aircraft simply disappeared. In 1943 six Wellington bombers, each carrying six men, took off from RAF Lossie for training flights over the North Sea and then just vanished.

Late in the war, in 1944 and 1945, a concentrated anti-shipping campaign was waged by RAF Strike Wings based at Boyndie and Dallachy. While the Mosquitoes and Beaufighters

flying from these Banffshire fields attacked U-boats and other
naval vessels, their main targets were the heavily guarded
cargo-ships that carried iron ore and other vital supplies
from northern Norway to the Third Reich. The fast-flying
Mosquitoes of the Banff Strike Wing were commanded by
the flamboyant Group Captain Max Aitken, son of Lord
Beaverbrook the newspaper proprietor and onetime member of
the War Cabinet. The slower Beaufighters flew from Dallachy,
and their aircrew, it needs to be stressed, were drawn as in all
the aerial campaigns from many different countries. The Strike
Wings based at Banff and Dallachy included, for instance,
Norwegian, New Zealand and Canadian squadrons. This writer,
who was at school at Buckie at the time, has vivid memories of
the twin-engined and heavily-armed Beaufighters circling over
the town until all the Dallachy planes were aloft. Then, as the
Wing flew off across the North Sea, they were joined by their
fighter escort, Mustangs that had flown over from Longside
field at Peterhead. While severe losses were inflicted on the
enemy, the allied air crews suffered many casualties. The losses
suffered by the Banffshire wings were in fact heavier than in
any other operational flying done by the RAF in the late stages
of the war. The author can recall too hearing from one of the
flight crew, who used to visit the family home, of one disastrous
day 'Black Friday' (9th February 1945) when Beaufighters from
the Dallachy Wing were 'jumped' by German fighters. Nine
of the Dallachy Beaufighters were destroyed also one of the
escorting Mustangs. To commemorate the achievements of the
men and women of Banff Strike Wing, a memorial stone cut —
most appropriately — from Norwegian granite was erected at
Boyndie in 1989. Dallachy too is to have a memorial — to be
unveiled in July 1992.

The Norwegian connection was shown in other ways.
Norwegian and British troops, stationed in the north-east,
underwent training in mountain warfare. The Cairngorms
was an ideal area for this specialised form of training. These
elaborate preparations were designed as a large-scale bluff
to try to convince the Germans that the Allies planned an
invasion of Norway. To help persuade the enemy that these
plans were serious, the British used a double agent to transmit
misleading radio messages. This was John Moe, one of two

'The Hillocks' — Ramsay Macdonald's residence at Lossiemouth.

Norwegians who were trained as secret agents and flown over to Scotland and landed, like the earlier trio, on the Banffshire coast. After landing at Crovie in April 1941, they speedily gave themselves up. Moe, who had no intention of serving the Germans, fed back misleading information gleaned, as his German spy masters supposed, from his base in Aberdeen.

Although airfields like Boyndie and Dallachy were eventually closed down, the air bases at Lossiemouth and Kinloss continued in use. Post-war Moray has derived considerable economic benefit from the presence of these major defence establishments, and the population of the towns and parishes most closely affected has risen. Local opinion in the 1950s, though, was that the service personnel were for the most part temporary residents with 'different roots, interests and occupations from the native inhabitants . . .' This view was echoed by Agnes Keith who, writing in 1975, described the impact of the Lossie base. 'The Air Station,' she wrote, 'brought much employment to Lossiemouth, and there has been a certain amount of intermarriage between English airmen and Lossiemouth girls, but it still remains an alien part of the parish, a separate community with its own churches and its own social life.'

This sense of separateness is manifest at election times. Whereas service personnel traditionally vote for the UK political parties, many of the Moray voters, as with those in Banffshire, have in recent years supported the Scottish National Party. It would seem that the Labour Party, at any rate, has not gained very much from the presence of the defence establishments. It must be said though, that outwith Aberdeen city, the north-east has never been fertile ground for Labour, although ironically the very first Labour Prime Minister, James Ramsay Macdonald, was a Lossie loon. Since he deserted Labour in 1931 to head a Tory-dominated National Government, he was not surprisingly denounced as a traitor and turncoat. His Labour successors, again not surprisingly, prefer to ignore the very considerable part he played in helping to build and shape their party. Although too easily dismissed as 'a boneless wonder', the stand that Ramsay Macdonald took in opposing British participation in the First World War was certainly both principled and courageous. The petty-minded patriots who insisted on his expulsion from Moray Golf Club did not see it in that light, however.

Despite the support that the Conservatives drew from the Moray air bases, the Moray constituency (and Banffshire too) was captured by the Nationalists in the SNP upsurge of the early 1970s. Previously both seats — once Liberal held — had been considered to be solidly Conservative and Unionist. Although the Conservatives won them back in 1979, the SNP triumphed in 1987. In the interim, the boundaries had been redrawn. Banffshire had disappeared as a separate seat, the western part going to Moray and the eastern being linked with Buchan. Since the Nationalists also held Angus, the north-east was, depending on one's standpoint, either the SNP's last redoubt or its springboard for future growth and expansion. In the April 1992 General Election, SNP retained their three north-eastern seats.

The rise of the SNP in this area is not altogether surprising since the north-east is one of the heartlands of traditional Scottish culture. Although many words have fallen into disuse, Scots, for instance, is still widely spoken. Certainly, as with Gaelic, Scots was often denigrated, and the ruling elite tried to eliminate the local dialect and forms of speech. In the

1830s many clergymen, for instance, anticipated that the local dialect, a 'vicious kind' of Scotch, would be 'improved by a more extended education and better qualified instructors'. Nevertheless, the Doric, as it is popularly termed, has stood up quite well. Since many Scottish words and expressions remain in everyday use it's certainly nae time tae beery (bury) it. So much of our written heritage is in Scots. Writers of genius like Elgin-born Jessie Kesson use the Doric. Our forefathers and precursors used the Doric in their everyday parlance. If you translate the pithy sayings of people like Geordie Roy into English, their character is diminished. Geordie Roy was a Kingston-on-Spey worthy of yesteryear whose adages and folk wisdom were recorded by a local historian. One of his functions was to intimate funerals. One villager, when informed about a sudden death, expressed his surprise. 'But surely,' he exclaimed, 'James Cruickshanks is nae dead: I saw him working on his land two days ago.' But Geordie soon settled the argument. 'Weel,' he remarked, 'that may or may not be: they're gaun tae beery him onywye.'

Just to be contrary, though, I shall conclude with verses by Sir Alexander Gray which, though written in English, encapsulate the sentiments of this particular exile.

'This is my country,
The land that begat me.
These windy spaces
Are surely my own,
And those that here toil
In the sweat of their faces
Are flesh of my flesh
And bone of my bone.'

Further Reading

Anon. *Macduff and its Harbour 1783–1966*, Macduff, 1966

J. R. Allan, *North-East Lowlands of Scotland*, Hale, 1952

R. C. Cant, *Old Elgin*, Elgin, 1946

R. C. Cant, *Old Moray*, Elgin, 1948

W. Cramond, *The Church and Churchyard of Cullen*, Aberdeen, 1883 (and many other titles by the same author)

V. Gaffney, *Tomintoul – its Glens and its People*, Sutherland Press, 1970

[J. Grant & W. Leslie], *Survey of the Province of Moray*, 1984 reprint by Moray District Libraries of 1798 original edition

G. Hutcheson, *Days of Yore*, 1979 reprint by Cluny Books of 1887 original edition

J. Hughes, 'A Steep Turn to the Stars: a History of Aviation in the Moray Firth', Benevenagh Books, 1991

A. Keith, *The Parish of Drainie and Lossiemouth*, 1975

C. Larner, *Enemies of God – The Witch-hunt in Scotland*, Chatto & Windus, 1981

P. Marren, *Grampian Battlefields*, Aberdeen University Press, 1990

C. McKean, *Banff and Buchan: An Illustrated Architectural Guide*, Mainstream, 1990

C. McKean, *The District of Moray: An Illustrated Architectural Guide*, Scottish Academic Press, 1987

J. M. Macpherson, *Primitive Beliefs in the North-East of Scotland*, Longmans, 1929

D. Omand, *The Moray Book*, Edinburgh, Paul Harris, 1976

I. Ralston & J. Inglis, *Foul Hordes: the Picts in the North-East and their background*, University of Aberdeen, 1984

C. Rampini, *A History of Moray and Nairn*, Blackwood, 1897

M. Seton, *Moray Past and Present*, Moray District Libraries, 1978

M. Seton, *Speyside Past and Present*, Moray District Libraries, 1984 (and many other titles by the same author published by Moray District Libraries)

I. A. G. Shepherd, *Exploring Scotland's Heritage: Grampian*, HMSO, 1986

I. A. G. Shepherd & I. B. M. Ralston, *Early Grampian*, Grampian Regional Council, 1979

D. J. Smith, *Action Stations 7. Military Airfields of Scotland, the North-East and Northern Ireland*, Patrick Stephens, 1989 edition

J. S. Smith and D. Stevenson *Fermfolk and Fisherfolk*, Aberdeen University Press, 1989

R. Smith, *One Foot in the Sea*, John Donald, 1991

R. Stewart, *Sail and Steam*, Moray District Libraries, 1986

D. Stevenson, *Alasdair MacColla and the Highland Problem in the Seventeenth Century*, John Donald, 1980

A. & H. Taylor, *Jacobites of Aberdeenshire and Banffshire in the Forty Five*, Aberdeen, 1928

W. Taylor, *The Military Roads in Scotland*, David & Charles, 1976

J. Thomas & D. Turnock, *A Regional History of the Railways of Great Britain*, Vol 15: *North of Scotland*, David & Charles, 1989

F. Thompson, *Discovering Speyside*, John Donald, 1990

P. Thompson, T. Wailey, & T. Lummis, *Living the Fishing*, Routledge & Kegan Paul, 1981

C. Wighton and G. Peiss, *They Spied on England*, Odhams, 1958 (Despite the appalling title, this book gives an accurate account of the 'Banffshire spies' affair.)

B. Wilkinson, *The Heilan Line*, Dornoch Press, 1988

Index